Disciple Maker
Crisis of Disobedience in the Evangelical Church

M. O. Buzz Williams

"The fruit of the righteous is a tree of life, and he who wins souls is wise,"

Proverbs 11:30

ISBN: 1461123054
ISBN-13: 978-1461123057

Dedication

This book is dedicated to my wife Carol, my family, and fellow disciple makers who have prayed and labored together with us through the years for the cause of His gospel.

Affirmation: Almighty God, the heavenly Father of Abraham, Isaac, and Israel is Holy, Holy, Holy. He is not slack concerning His word or His promises. His word will not return unto Him void, but it shall accomplish all that He planned from the beginning.

His mercy is exceedingly great and He is strong to save all who call upon Him in repentance of sin and faith in His only begotten Son, Christ Jesus.

Vision

"Righteousness exalts a nation, but sin is a reproach to any people," Proverbs 14:34. It is with much regret that many thousands of Evangelical Churches have closed their doors in the United States in our lifetime. But it is also encouraging that our hope is in the Lord Jesus Christ who is able to revive His Church.

The recent decades have produced many in Church leadership who attempt to supplant His righteousness with a determined focus and emphasis on social justice. That other gospel ignores the sin problem, God's grace, the substitutionary atonement of Jesus, His bodily resurrection from the dead, and His command to make disciples.

This book exposes the fog of deception, moves beyond the status quo, and explains what has been made available to every Evangelical Church.

God's method is sublime. His timing is perfect. You have the means at your fingertips, the Bible, the word of God. Call upon Him who the scriptures describe as always faithful. His ear is not deaf, His eye is not dim, and His love for His children never fails.

Call upon Him while there is still time. First be a disciple and then a disciple maker, edify the local Church, and expect to greatly enlarge your ministry for His glory. "The fruit of the righteous is a tree of life, and he who wins souls is wise," Proverbs 11:30.

Introduction

I venture on this book not knowing how I shall communicate to you the significance of the command from our Lord to "Go, therefore, and make disciples of all nations..." Matthew 28:19. Those who understand this command, and are obedient to it, already have assurance it is given on Christ's authority! My attempt in this treatise to impart the necessity for obedience to, and urgency of, this command are entrusted to the Holy Spirit, who alone is able to revive the Evangelical Church ["Church"] in the United States.

Regrettably, the Church in our country, for the most part, has either deliberately set aside or neglected the Great Commission commanded by our Lord. It is glaringly evident throughout America, where once numerous, formerly vibrant, God-fearing congregations thrived, that these Churches have since defaulted in their responsibility for making disciples. This has apparently occurred by reason of gross rebellion or neglect in large part by Church leadership.

Devastating results are evident from the rapid decline of the Church in America during the last fifty years. Through reasonable observation one may accurately conclude the Church lacks a consistent, godly-influence on the American government, and on the country as a whole. Salt and light are rare in American culture!

The truth, to varying degrees, is admittedly taught from some Church pulpits, Sunday school classes, and Bible studies. However, limiting the teaching of Scriptural truth without the teaching of God's grace generally results in self–serving legalism. Sin is not seriously and biblically confronted in many contemporary pulpit sermons. Why? It is thought by many in Church leadership that some Church members might become uncomfortable. Congregations, therefore, do not progress spiritually from milk to meat. Not surprisingly, Church discipline all but disappears. Amusement emanates from the pulpit and various forms of entertainment are used to fill the void on Sunday morning. Consequently, the impetus for disciple making lessens in importance and eventually becomes obscure.

The truth apart from grace tends to obscure God's full and complete redemptive work. It is by God's grace that our sin was dealt with through His Son's shed blood at Calvary. Disciple making is the means of grace used by God for building up the Church, broadcasting the gospel, winning souls, and contending for the faith within our country. It is now, therefore, in view of this crisis of disobedience, a critical time in our nation's history. Each Church leader ought to examine himself carefully. Church leaders ultimately determine what their commitment to the disciple-making ministry is going to be within their Church, and in their Jerusalem. Assuredly, it will ultimately determine the course of spiritual liberty in the United States.

Forward

"We hold these truths to be self-evident, that all men are created equal, that they are endowed by their Creator with certain unalienable rights, that among these are life, liberty and the pursuit of happiness." "Declaration of Independence," Thomas Jefferson, July 4, 1776 A.D.

Not surprisingly, the teaching of essential truths enumerated in the Declaration of Independence and the United States Constitution is very limited in our public schools. Graduating high school seniors, in most of America, have very limited understanding of our founding documents. Additionally, since 1961, the government has banned the teaching of Holy Scripture in the public schools. That decision by the Supreme Court resulted in the elimination of the freedom of choice by students for optional religious instruction. Religious instruction had formerly been available to public school students since before 1776 and continued up to 1961. The free exercise of choice for religious instruction became the target of a blind judiciary, which was aided by liberals whose calculated political ambitions were to tear down what our founding fathers had given us.

That flagrant lunge for power by progressives, disguised in secularism, dealt American society, and particularly America's posterity, a serious blow from which doctor Billy Graham responded, "America may never recover!" Our individual liberty is no longer believed to be a gift of God, but a prerogative of government, as most public school students seem to understand it today. As a regular substitute teacher in two high schools in

Alabama, it is my view that we citizens have become little more than pawns of the statist. Consequently, various forms of secular teaching, humanistic philosophy, and anti-Jew and anti-Christian rhetoric have become normative in American public schools.

Who can deny the wind of unbridled greed and all manner of ungodliness that has been sown via American politics in unprecedented measures since that ruling by the Court? Simultaneously, wolves continue to creep into Church leadership positions and the laity slumbers, dreaming that America will be exempt from the wrath to come. There are a few exceptions, but most main-line Churches are not fighting from the pulpit with the truth and grace of the gospel of Jesus, nor are they raising the biblical standard of God in their community, "…Be holy, for I Am holy," 1st Peter 1:16.

Church leaders, men who are charged to be watchmen, apparently are satisfied to be merely spectators in society. They are overwhelmingly negligent of their responsibility to their membership to first become a disciple and then disciple makers. They watch in vain, not knowing or understanding there is a whirlwind gathering in our nation! Disciple making is something contemporary leadership contends "it is not ready for at this time." It is necessary to admonish those leaders saying, "Nor will you ever be ready, because it requires prayer, and active, sacrificial obedience to God to make disciples!" Most Church leaders, in recent decades, did not train and deploy disciples or disciple-makers. The Church's long-standing negligence in America did much to aid the loss of individual religious liberty. What is your part, as a Church leader, in the solution to this crisis of disobedience in the Evangelical Church?

Contents

Acknowledgements

I thank all those many witnesses who have demonstrated the gospel of our Lord Jesus Christ in a diligent, consistent manner for my edification. Now I too fish in many seas:

Janice L. Mitchell, a prayerful sister, loving me and my family beyond what we deserve
Anna J. Williams, my mother, a humble, faithful prayer warrior and Godly example
Carl Rehkop, who winsomely encouraged me to attend Sunday school in the 1940(s)

Henrietta Fey, sixth-grade teacher who lovingly taught the Bible in the Public schools
Gabe Green, a church Elder who led by a quiet, consistent, Godly example
Manford George Gutzke, who openly wrestled obstinate men for the gospel's sake

Bert Anderson, who led me to a saving decision of faith in Jesus and repentance of sin
Ben Hayden, who faithfully taught the awesome Creator and His perfect holiness
Don Patterson, who loved my family and me into First Presby. Church, Jackson, MS

Bill Long, M.D., who regarded all our children as important to the kingdom of God
Luder Whitlock, who as a disciple maker, sought the greatest glory for the Lord
Andy Toth, missionary, whose life demonstrated reliance on the faithfulness of God

Val & Mildred Surgis, whose love drew my family to know unconditional compassion

Bruce Wideman, who taught me how to bring my Dad to a saving decision in Jesus

Bert Walker, M.D., alive to Christ, family physician, friend, exhorter, example to others

Bill Krug, who emphasized biblical precepts and God's grace found in Jesus' atonement

Frank M. Barker. Jr., who is diligent to follow Jesus into our Jerusalem to fish for men

Lance Radbill, a Jew, who called me into Christian discipleship and then disciple making

Ron Steele, who prayerfully taught many disciples and led us into disciple making

D. James Kennedy, who first made of himself a loving disciple before teaching others

Kennedy Smartt, who understands the essentials and exemplifies being a disciple maker

Parker Glasgow, who is my selfless prayer supporter and a tireless Jonathan at heart

Phillip Capra, who with quiet excitement, taught Christian apologetics to all the brethren

Richard Trucks, who demonstrated and encouraged sacrifice for the gospel of our Lord

Jeff Lowman, who taught Holy Scripture with joy and demonstrable conviction

Bud Newbold, who discipled others and encouraged my vision for disciple making

Bill Gray, who by example, would not compromise on Holy Scripture's Truth & Grace

Bill Buck, a brother whose hope and joy is in the Lord, and he cannot contain it

Jerry Sharpe, missionary, a humble and loving friend; disciple maker of many Asians
Sadie Custer, missionary, who greatly encouraged me to prayer petition and intercession
Harry Lange, stalwart friend, encourager, prayer warrior, and evangelist
Charles Stanley, who consistently teaches the sovereignty and love of God
Robert Garrison, who in difficult times, assures me of the leading of the Holy Spirit

Chapter 1

Children of the 1940(s) and 1950(s) in America

There were in the Churches of Carbondale, Pennsylvania, in the 1940(s) and 1950(s), a great multitude of citizens who regularly attended Sunday school classes. In those days, there were many more people in America who attended Sunday school, than there were people who attended the Church services. This experience is attested to by many folks older and wiser than me, and who unapologetically desire to see it again.

Sunday school was very interesting to most folks because questions could be asked by everyone and anyone without ridicule. People seemed to want to know the truth of Holy Scripture. Multitudes of Americans were greatly encouraged and responsive to Bible teaching and preaching. The typical American generally seemed to have an attitude of concern for their neighborhoods. People appeared to be helpful to one another. Used clothing was routinely handed down within the family and subsequently to their neighbors. Fruit and vegetables were commonly shared from neighborhood gardens by regular folks in many communities, Church affiliation notwithstanding.

Most young folks avoided serious trouble because it brought shame to one's self, their family, and their neighborhood. The tone of behavior in most American communities was greatly influenced by a long–standing, Judeo–Christian heritage.

The heathen, generally speaking, seemed to be influenced by the unfettered freedom of religious belief and enthusiasm of people who unabashedly wanted to share their testimonies and faith. Because of this, the Spirit of God seemed to greatly restrain even those who were un-churched.

If your schoolteacher suggested that he or she might want to contact your parents concerning your behavior or grades, then a certain justifiable fear gripped the student. It was clearly not what a student wanted to hear, because in most cases, corporal punishment, inflicted by your parents, was not uncommon.

The student was also subject to the paddle as a means of discipline in the public school. There tended to be a climate of respect in most academic environments due to this practice. Use of corporal punishment fostered a greater respect by students for their teachers, other adults, students, and public and private property in general. "Foolishness is bound up in the heart of a child; the rod of correction will drive it far from him," Proverbs 22:15.

Routinely, cars and trucks were often parked with keys left in the ignition. Why? It was the easiest place where you could find the keys to your vehicle! Besides, car theft was at a minimum in those days. Small towns and even larger cities did not seem to have the weighty volume of serious crime that we have today. Many people did not lock their doors to their homes when they went to market or away for the weekend. Neighbors typically looked out for the homes and property of others. Generally, your home was respected and not disturbed. Neighbors commonly demonstrated concern for each other. Multitudes of young folks in those days, unafraid, would stick out their thumb and hitchhike on the public highways from one town to another because of a generous and thoughtful American public.

Was there serious crime in those days? You bet! But specific sin and serious crime was also being confronted in the pulpit of the local church in general, and by law enforcement in particular. Moreover, the public schools were generally intolerant of rude behavior. Overall, the spiritual and ethical tone of America had not yet sunk to unimagined lows. Apathy by parents; ingratitude, rebellion, rude behavior, and gross indifference by students had not, as yet, gained its cold-blooded grip on American culture.

It was by no means a perfect world. Vile racial segregation existed. Ethnic distinction among some folks was a serious, spiritual, and cultural stumbling block. But at the same time, it was a world where people were encouraged in their own personal spiritual growth without government intrusion. The combined efforts of churches and schools to teach Scriptural truths reached millions of young people. It greatly helped society from sinking to its lowest common denominator.

The free exercise of religious freedom was prominent in most communities and in public schools. It was obviously both a direct and indirect source of blessing. Fundamentally, it was very beneficial in various aspects of American family life and society in general. The politicians seemed to take notice that Americans had higher levels of expectation from their representatives in government. The tenor of moral influence on American culture, because of the Church's influence and religious instruction taught in the public school, was far-reaching and enlightening to say the least.

It was not uncommon that money found in the street was returned to the owner. People were quick to help their neighbors. Children and women could move about, for the most part, without being molested or even worried about it. The routine in most neighbor-hoods was such that children could leave their bicycles in the park or in the front yard without them being stolen. America had its many faults, but we, the children of that generation, were the recipients of abundant blessings handed down from our founding fathers.

The Role of the Church and School

Importantly, the influence of vibrant local Churches, complimented by religious freedom exercised within the public schools, was the perpetual underpinning of spiritual and moral strength for a nation dependent upon God as envisioned by our founding fathers.

Students, it seemed, were always ready to share or explain their religious beliefs and there was not any interference by government. Political correctness did not rule the thinking of our day. Patriotism was in vogue.

Authentic Religious Liberty

World War One, World War Two, and the Korean War veterans were held in high esteem. We were proud of them and grateful for their individual sacrifice for us personally. Consequently, many patriots answered the call to arms during the Vietnam War. We served because it was thought to be our duty and we wanted to preserve American liberty and freedom for all citizens, just as others did for us.

The influence of religious freedom permeated our society. The local Methodist, Episcopal, Baptist, Presbyterian, Greek, and Russian Orthodox, Roman Catholic Churches, and Synagogues, etc. were often full to overflowing.

The public schools in our town, not unlike other towns in Pennsylvania and other states, had an optional religious instruction class every week. The last class on Wednesday afternoon was typically reserved for that purpose. Each student was free to choose to go to study hall or to go to the religious instruction class of his or her choice.

Teachers volunteered to teach religious instruction classes. The local Rabbi, Pastor and Priest made themselves available to all students. The decision to attend any particular religious instruction class was left to the student and to the student's family. Study hall was an option to those not wanting religious instruction, though I don't recall anyone who would prefer it to the alternative.

The free exercise of religion or the free choice of religious instruction, for the student, family, and school faculty was alive and well in America at that time. It was authentic religious liberty!

After all, students and faculty were citizens too! Should students and teachers have the freedom to choose religious instruction under the free exercise clause of the Constitution, without coercion by the federal government, and without being forced into the religion of secularism? At that time, there was no federal mandate or misapplication of the Fourteenth Amendment by the Supreme Court to the states that prohibited the freedom of choice by students for religious instruction in the public schools.

The obvious moral and cultural impact of religious instruction classes benefited the community because it set the cultural tone of our personal relationships.

It also made one aware of our blessings due to the sacrifice of others.

The exercise of religion undeniably fostered appreciation and gratitude for what was freely given to us all. Honorable behavior and righteousness exalted our communities, towns, cities, the forty-eight states, and our nation in those days.

In God We Trust

"Congress shall make no law respecting an establishment of religion, or prohibiting the free exercise thereof…," <u>United States Constitution,</u> 1776. Incidentally, The Supreme Court of the United Sates, in recent years, admittedly, has acknowledged Secularism to be a religion, and it is still taught by fiat in the public schools! The founding fathers of our nation expressed themselves in a manner contrary to what the contemporary American government espouses today as evidenced in the following historical testimonies:

George Washington, "It is the duty of a nation to acknowledge the providence of Almighty God, to obey His will, to be grateful for its benefits, and humbly to implore His protection and favor."

John Adams, "We have no government armed with power capable of contending with human passions unbridled by morality and religion. Our Constitution was made only for a moral and religious people. It is wholly inadequate to the government of any other."

Thomas Jefferson, "And can the liberties of a nation be thought secure when we have removed their only firm basis, a conviction in the minds of the people that these liberties are of the gift of God? That they are not to be violated but with His wrath? Indeed I tremble for my country when I reflect that God is just; that His justice cannot sleep forever."

Benjamin Franklin, "I've lived, sir, a long time. And the longer I live, the more convincing proofs I see of this truth: That God governs in the affairs of men. If a sparrow cannot fall to the ground without His notice, is it probable that an empire cannot rise without His aid? We've been assured in the sacred writings that unless the Lord builds the house, they labor in vain who build it."

Some disciple makers, to their credit today, have chosen to diligently work in the home-schooling environment. The home school, generally speaking, appears to have a better track record than the public school in terms of academic achievement and religious [spiritual] training.

A few very wise Americans carried their vision for disciple making into the non-government Christian classical schools [Classical schools]. The Classical schools generally impart a biblical world-life view with Christ-centered teaching of every academic subject. Within the arena of school sports and academic competition, students in the Classical schools typically practice what they were taught in religious instruction.

Not surprisingly, results typically show that the public schools are generally not comparable to the Classical schools, but leagues below in academic achievement, logic, and religious [spiritual] training. The Church school, in some instances, has progressed similarly to Classical schools, although sadly, both schools are few and far between. Economics or the ability to pay for a Church school or Classical school education deters many students from attending these institutions.

The Pilgrims and subsequently many colonists in early America understood that catechism and religious instruction is a means to strengthen the family unit, the community, and the nation.

Sadly, catechizing of whole families by Churches is generally neglected today. Many Churches do not teach catechism except in the lower elementary grades. That is, many that do teach catechism tend to limit the training to students and do not teach adults or whole families.

The exercise of authentic religious freedom by colonists would someday encourage many people of various denominations to support the values expressed in our nation's founding documents. It fortified their resolve as a new nation under God. Even so, the children of the 1940(s) and 1950(s) were ultimately beneficiaries of authentic religious freedom.

Chapter 2

The Decline of the Evangelical Church in America

Attempting to teach partial truth and omitting grace cannot impart understanding about the undeserved love of God, whom the Scriptures describe as "...Holy, Holy, Holy," Revelation 4:8.

"Truth without grace crushes people and ceases to be truth... Grace without truth degenerates into deceitful tolerance... Truth hates sin... Grace loves sinners... Those full of grace and truth do both," "The Grace and Truth Paradox," Randy Alcorn, page 88.

The evidentiary fact is Church leadership, in most American communities, refuses to go into their own Jerusalem, first as a ready witness or disciple, and secondly in the capacity of a disciple maker for the training of its own congregational membership.

Some might ask, "How is this refusal by Church leadership evident in the Church?"

The leadership may assent to send missionaries to Samaria and the uttermost parts of the world. They may even encourage us to write a check to support that effort. Certainly, this is necessary for the support of missionaries. The leadership may also authorize and promote the teaching of a Sunday school class on evangelism. Some leaders may infrequently engage in short-term mission trips of a week or two.

But more often than not, Church leadership stops short of qualifying their members and holding them accountable in sustained ministry training in order that they may become disciples and then disciple makers. It's just expecting Church leadership to do too much! It's certainly not popular nor is it convenient.

Not Counting the Cost

Therefore, with respect to making a commitment to disciple making, expectation levels for most men in Church leadership gravitate somewhere between the ankle-low to a knee-high position. The leadership expectations fall short! It is a problem of the heart!

The result is "passive evangelism," or disciple making in "low-gear." This half – hearted, less than serious attempt to engage Church members as witnesses, disciples and disciple makers in one's own congregation cannot pass as sincere obedience in time of spiritual warfare.

The low-gear approach to disciple making does not call for Christian soldiers who are teachable, responsible, accountable, committed, and ready for deployment. Passive evangelism and low-gear evangelism neither requires the layperson to count the cost, nor to take up his cross.

Failing to Love and Lead

The leadership, in most Churches, purposely avoids demonstrating disciple making to its membership. They avoid training their members on how to winsomely engage others in their daily rounds for the purpose of sharing their own testimony or even the Gospel of our Redeemer in way-of-life ministry.

Think about it! How many leaders in your Church, especially Pastors, Elders and Deacons, actually engage in regular, active witnessing and the sharing of the gospel of our Lord outside the Church building, with the intent of winning souls and demonstrating disciple making to church members? I would be surprised if the number is more than 3% of the leadership based on my own experience.

How many of our Church leaders routinely lead church members through regular discipleship clinics? How many Church leaders are engaged in active disciple making as part of their ministry? In short, most of the Church leadership in America fails miserably in disciple making as it only talks, and then fails to act in love or by grace!

More Like the World

I would not diminish the importance of Christian fellowship. However, there is magnified emphasis on the "sense of community" within the local church that often obscures the urgency of becoming a disciple or that of becoming a disciple maker.

Not infrequently, Churches at a cost of millions of dollars build large community centers. While the centers are maintained for the benefit of the local members, the majority of these community centers contribute almost nothing toward witnessing, evangelism, and intentional disciple making. Intentional training in disciple making, by Church leadership, is missing in their plans!

Social–based programs occupy much of the Church member's time and overwhelmingly these programs become priority one in many Churches. The Church of yesteryear, in many instances, has become the YMCA of today. That is, in my view, most members of the YMCA actually join for things other than becoming involved in a Bible study or to receive training as a disciple and then as a disciple maker.

People typically join the YMCA for basketball, handball, bowling, swimming, tennis, etc. But how many attend the YMCA today for Bible study and active disciple making? Many Churches too have changed their ministry thrust. Rather that proclaiming Christ crucified, it is now therefore in competition with the local YMCA to draw neighbors into its "community center."

Passive Discipleship

Disciple making, in reality, appears all but forgotten by Church leadership. We will acknowledge some positive evangelistic outreach in community centers and the YMCA here, but evangelism is not disciple making! Evangelism is, however, an integral part of disciple making!

At best, most Church leaders exercise or encourage a "passive" discipleship. But ordinary Church members typically don't confront folks intentionally. That is, they do not ask permission to share their testimony or the gospel outside of Church, at least not with any regularity.

However, if someone should ask the typical Church member about their faith, then they might possibly share what they know. That is to say, they might think about their personal testimony for a while, because they were never heretofore guided in the thoughtful development of one.

They may attempt to share the gospel with an inquirer, though perhaps their Church leadership did not give them serious training on this important matter, other than what was imparted by way of a sermon or Bible study. Besides, most congregation members seem to think that sharing the gospel is the Pastor's job anyway!

The majority of Churches today, who claim to be evangelical, do not intentionally train their members how to develop their own a personal testimony. Likewise, they do not teach their members how to share the gospel of our Lord. It certainly is not politically correct to do so! And it is just not done in most Churches.

It is as though the Church leadership is ashamed to equip their members! Are we surprised that our leadership does not provide that kind of training? Should we dare ask about it? Though the command to make disciples is over two thousand years old, the sorry excuse typically given by Church leadership is, "We're just not ready for that as a Church!"

Ignoring the Command to "Go"

The real reason is they do not want to do it! The next time you are in Sunday school try asking the class, "How many intentionally, or otherwise, attempted to give your testimony for your faith this week, outside of the Church? How many shared the gospel this month, outside the Church?" Not surprisingly, the results in a typical class, based on my experience, generally run near zero to a high of 3%.

The biblical model for disciple making is Jesus. "Then He said to them, follow Me and I will make you fishers of men," Matthew 4:19. Prayer fills the cup of petition. The Holy Spirit opens the door of opportunity, gives you an appointment with someone, provides an audience for the trusting disciple, and then He puts the words of Jesus in your mouth. "And I have put My words in your mouth..." Isaiah 51:16.

Then with conviction enough to follow Him in obedience, the Lord uses the faithful messenger and the gospel to win souls. Yes, the Lord uses His own as the means to lead others to Himself! The result is always for His glory, and the disciple's joy is being made full in Him. "But now I come to You, and these things I speak in the world, that they may have My joy fulfilled in themselves," John 17:13.

Those in leadership positions in the Church today, for reasons not biblical, which routinely ignore the command to make disciples, are unearthing consequences that are detrimental to the Church, the family, and the nation! The Apostle Paul explained to his disciple, Timothy, "And the things you have heard from me among many witnesses, commit these to faithful men who will be able to teach others also," 2nd Timothy 2:2.

Disciple Making is Not Optional

Disobedience is sin! Sin is rebellion and it always has consequences; not just for us as individuals but as families and as communities of believers. Sin damages our personal testimony as believers and it ultimately damages our nation. It leaves a sad and shameful legacy for our children and grandchildren.

A Puritan Pastor exhorted the clergy in his day, "And, thus, I have given you those reasons which forced me to publish, in plain English, so much of the sins of the ministry... But I find it impossible to avoid offending those who are at once guilty and impenitent; for there is no way of avoiding this, but by our silence, or their patience: and silent we cannot be, because of their guilt and impenitence. But plain dealers will always be approved in the end; and the time is at hand when you will confess that they were your best friends," "The Reformed Pastor" Richard Baxter, page 41.

Nevertheless, there is a remnant! The Lord Jesus is able to complete all that He has purposed for them that are His. "…Just as He chose us in Him before the foundation of the world…" Ephesians 1:4a. His purpose was determined before the foundation of the world. His call to obedience for you and me cannot be separated from disciple making. "He who has my commandments and keeps them, it is he who loves Me. And he who loves Me will be loved by My Father, and I will love him and manifest Myself to him," John 14:21. "Go therefore and make disciples of all the nations…" Matthew 28:19a.

Discipleship and disciple making are not an optional extra for the man or woman of God. No special talent, rank, or political position is required to be His disciple. Notice, "For you see your calling, brethren, that not many wise according to the flesh, not many mighty, not many noble are called," 1st Corinthians 1:26.

Available and Useable

God the Holy Spirit delights in using the person of humility and contrition to accomplish His holy purpose as testified of in Holy Scripture. It is in His grace and in His revealed word that all sufficiency abounds. Our joy is full in knowing the Truth, and by knowing and by experiencing the grace of God. We are called to make ourselves available to follow Him, first as disciples,

because He first loved us, and then as disciple makers
who are faithful to train others, because we love Him.

Henry Blackaby explained, "The Holy Spirit and the
Word of God will instruct you and help you know
when and where God is working. Once you know
where He is working, you will adjust your life to join
Him where He is working," "<u>Experiencing God</u>,"
Henry T. Blackaby & Claude V. King, page 15.
"...My Father has been working until now, and I have
been working. ...Most assuredly, I say to you, the Son
can do nothing of Himself; but what He sees the Father
do; for whatever He does, the Son also does in like
manner. For the Father loves the Son and shows Him
all things that He Himself does; and He will show Him
greater works than these, that you may marvel," John
5:17, 19-20.

It is imperative that we in the evangelical Church follow
Jesus as the biblical model in becoming a disciple and
then becoming a disciple maker.

As one sinner redeemed by the saving blood of the
Lamb of God, I humbly submit that I have great joy in
knowing that as I make myself available to the Lord; He
has made me useable on multiple occasions! It
confirms for me what the hymn writer says, "How
marvelous, how wonderful, is my Savior's love for me!"
His glory and His gospel is my focus and I have learned
that disciple making is always found in the path of
obedience.

Communicating truth and grace found only in Jesus is
the principal thing. "We beheld His glory, the glory as

of the only begotten of the Father, full of grace and truth," John 1:14. You have heard that it is written, "For I am the Lord, I do not change," Malachi 3:6. He is the same yesterday, today and forever. In Him alone are our redemption, purpose, significance, life, eternal security, joy, and exceeding great reward!

Depravity in the Visible Church

During the Eisenhower administration, about 1954, it seemed, to many folks, that the nation had moved into a responsible era of government. President Eisenhower proposed and Congress approved that, "One nation under God," be added to our Pledge of Allegiance to the flag of the United States.

The Church became relaxed, less watchful, and took occasion to slumber. Things were not as they appeared. Wolves in sheep's clothing moved into places of leadership within every denomination of the Church.

The wolves saw opportunities to fill the positions of Pastor, Elder, or Deacon with like-minded leaders. The acceptance of progressivism or liberalism became a creeping cancer in the Church. Many liberal Pastors questioned the authority and sufficiency of Scripture. Likewise, liberalism grew and permeated many governmental institutions.

The Church today has a less-than-positive influence on government because of its own record of disobedience. Many Church leaders have become openly indifferent to the teachings of Scriptural doctrine. Basic presuppositions formerly gleaned from Scripture are ignored and, therefore, the moral moorings of the Church eroded.

Time would yield evidence of an inward depravity that influenced the Church in America. The government in the United States too was adrift. Society and government over time would begin to call good evil and evil good as their personal preferences took precedence over biblical precepts.

Most people who claimed to be Protestants or evangelical were ill-equipped to deal with abortion, homosexuality, adultery, fornication, pornography, drugs and gambling, let alone adherence to the command to honor your parents, or love your neighbor as you love yourself. It seemed, as in the days of Noah, men were doing what was right in their own eyes.

A spiritual void gradually enveloped much of American society and progressivism grew unchecked throughout academia. Institutions of higher learning, formerly founded by Christian Churches, became the breeding ground for liberalism. Liberalism offered students a permissive freedom to do what they wanted without any moral compunction.

The Price of Religious Liberty

The first rule of liberalism and progressivism is, of course, there is no god! Liberalism, without exception, ignores real freedom. Real freedom is doing what you ought to do; that is to say, doing what God commands in Holy Scripture. Liberalism is at enmity with God and corrupts any society it touches.

Not surprising, in subsequent years, Liberalism, Progressivism, Socialism, Marxism, and Communism accelerated their ideological assault against our democratic republic and representative government. The infiltration by the enemy also expanded within the Church by various methods, some more subtle than others.

Basic tenants of freedom and individual liberty are proclaimed in the Declaration of Independence, the Constitution of the United States of America, and further explained in the "Federalist Papers." These founding documents are unparalleled in history and are the basis for our liberty as American citizens.

The founding fathers advocated free markets, entrepreneurship through hard work, personal responsibility, limited government, liberty and self-determination for each individual. Freedom and liberty, endowed by Nature's God, the Creator, was declared to be the groundwork for our new country.

America would rise to an economic, philanthropic, and military plateau the world has never before seen. "For everyone to whom much is given, from him much will be required..." Luke 12:48b.

American free enterprise, not the government, invented the light bulb, the automobile assembly line, the telephone, the airplane, the transistor, the computer, modern life-saving medicine, and an unparalleled standard of living the world has never before known. The stewardship responsibility for protecting that standard of living, and our individual rights, is inextricably linked to the conscientious, deliberate effort of each citizen to understand and vote on important issues.

The stewardship responsibility of religious liberty is not any less important within the Church. The response to the command to love God with all our heart, mind, soul and strength and then to love our neighbor as ourselves slipped farther away, albeit very gradually, an inch at a time, over the years. All the while, most of the Church slumbered.

Thomas Jefferson warned his new nation, "The price of liberty is eternal vigilance!" Limited federal government, the sovereignty of each state, and individual rights ought to be taught and understood by the people. Liberty would not be easily kept! It carries an awesome responsibility. Liberty and freedom is not typically lost by miles, but by inches.

Jefferson explained in the "Declaration of Independence," "We hold these truths to be self - evident, that all men are created equal, that they are endowed by their Creator [God] with certain unalienable rights that among these are life, liberty and the pursuit of happiness."

The first Congress of the United States paid for, produced and distributed 4,000 Bibles for the public schools in the 13 new states. Two of the 54 framers of the Constitution were Deists, Thomas Jefferson and Benjamin Franklin. The other 52 were devout professing Christians, 29 of whom were seminary graduates. All 54 men, to a man, pledged their lives, their sacred honor and fortunes to the end that America would be free of an overbearing, ponderous, central government, foreign or domestic.

Abraham Lincoln, years later, would reinforce this theme, "…That this nation, under God, shall have a new birth of freedom… a government of, by, and for the people." Gettysburg Address, Abraham Lincoln, November 19, 1863.

Populism Replaces Disciple Making

During the 1940(s) and 1950(s) many folks began to dabble with palm reading, séances, Ouija boards, crystal-ball reading, and horoscopes. Not that it was never done before, but it took on a more commercial cloak, became publically acceptable, and of course, it was just for fun. It was in those same years that the bad guys in the movies literally wore black hats. Most American citizens would not go to the movies on Sunday.

Matter of fact, over 95% of the stores in our town would not open for business on Sunday. Church bells rang out on Sunday morning to call citizens throughout the city to worship God.

There seemed to be a populism that competed with precepts that were taught in Sunday school classes. America was getting mixed messages from its culture. Because the Church was weakened in its teaching, preaching, and disciple making, a defiant, rebellious streak sprang up in American culture. Many Churches would abdicate from catechizing its members and from making disciples. Pulpit oratory and populism was now in vogue.

Losing Religious Liberty

Disappointingly, by 1961-2 a very liberal Supreme Court rendered decisions that religious education, the Bible, and prayer had no place in the public schools. Loosely translated, the rationale was that teachers worked for the government. If teachers taught religious education, then there would be a state [national] sponsorship of religion. This was, of course, deception by a shrewd and very clever enemy.

The free exercise of choice for students to choose to go to any religious instruction class or not, was now illegal. Prayer was considered an offense by a small minority and, therefore, the federal government would not tolerate it. The United States government expelled God from the public educational institutions! Secularism became the new religion of the public schools. The Supreme Court in America had deliberately thrown out both prayer and the Bible. An identical result occurred in Austria when approximately 98% of its citizens invited Hitler into their government around 1938. The Austrians had almost 25% unemployment; young people went door–to–door begging for food. They observed that Germany had full employment and free health care. Why not become part of the German empire?

An immediate result of the decision by the people of Austria to come under the authority of Germany was the elimination of any religious instruction in the public schools! Almost overnight, the cross of Christ and Star of David were very quickly replaced in the public schools with the swastika and a picture of the Fuher, a.k.a., Adolph Hitler.

Worldly Influence on the Church

The year 1973 saw a new low in the moral fabric of America! A narrow block of Christians were shocked by it. Many who professed to be Christians were not informed and, therefore, unable to articulate a biblical world-life view on the subject of abortion. The Supreme Court effectually held in Roe verses Wade that a fetus, healthy or not, had no right-to-life. American law now devalued human life.

Soon enough, the rate-of-divorce from Christian marriages skyrocketed and, therefore, paralleled the divorce rate of secular America. Men and women were not held to biblical account, or disciplined by the Church, for divorce or for the abortion of a healthy baby where the life of the mother was not in jeopardy.

The Church was ill prepared because most of its leadership themselves lacked biblical training and conviction. Most Church congregations, by fiat, were liberal in their views. The absence of watchful leadership and the absence of disciple making by leadership began to erode the testimony of the Church.

Political correctness aided the confused, liberal Church member by excusing him or her from taking any moral stand. "After all it's only a fetus," became the cry from the liberal leadership and it was echoed by the liberal membership of the Church. Nevertheless, fetus is a Latin word for a small child. But why confuse the liberal Church leader or liberal congregation with facts?

Enter more political correctness. The term "gay" was a familiar and often used term without perverted connation prior to the 1960(s). Gay, as applied to homosexuals, purposely misdirects criticism of a perverted lifestyle. After all, where in Holy Scripture is there any criticism of gay? "Don't ask, don't tell" would later become government policy that tends to overlook the serious consequences of perversion in the ranks of the military.

Honorable men despise the hypocrisy of political correctness and moral turpitude that subverts our nation's moral integrity. Sin is sin! It is not a question or interpretation of what the definition of is "is!"

Ignoring the God of the Bible

The lack of biblical teaching by Churches, in general, has led to further decay within the American culture. Fewer Churches are having Sunday evening worship service. Many Churches do not have a mid-week Church service for families and singles, nor do children and whole families receive sustained catechism training. There may be a choir rehearsal, Church dinner, or perhaps a few Bible studies here and there, but many Churches mostly ignore serious probing into biblical precepts.

Disappointingly, most Pastors don't visit in the homes of their members at least once a year. Personal relationships between the leadership and membership, in most Churches, tend to be very thin at best.

The youth ministry in many instances is not challenging to the degree that young people ever practice their own testimony, learn Scriptural passages, or learn a basic gospel presentation. However, the greater problem that can be observed is a lack of mature, committed leadership in the Church.

Interestingly, some Senior Pastors prefer a younger leadership that will stay in line with a prescribed agenda. A spiritually mature leadership is perceived by some Senior Pastors to be a threat, especially if experienced leaders espouse the notion of disciple making.

We know from Scripture, that Israel turned its back on God through its disobedience during Elijah's time. Sin was convenient at that time for politicians and for Church leadership. Today the sins of homosexuality and convenient abortion, where there is actually no danger to the life of the mother involved, are symptoms of a greater sin against God.

The Hebrew TENAK, or Christian Old Testament, describes how sin ultimately affects children's behavior as evidenced in the life of Absalom. Absalom publicly defied his father, David, and planned to murder him for his throne. Francis Schaeffer, with reference to 2 Samuel 15, explained, "Absalom was a man of anti-law in the same spirit as the coming Antichrist," "No Little People," page 138. Multitudes of leaders in the Church and, likewise, in the American government ignore the God of the Bible. Some call themselves Reverend,

Pastor, Bishop, Teacher, Elder or Deacon and some are called Senator, Representative, Judge or President. Many of them publically defy the God of Abraham, Isaac, and Israel through their political correctness, their vote, and their individual quest for authority and power.

Seeing, Yet Not Understanding

The government of the United States of America, in the name of fairness, sanctions witches or wicken as a religion in the military establishment. Our current President proclaimed recently to the world that, "The United States of America is not a Christian country!" "...Is it because there is no God in Israel [or America] that you are going to inquire of Baal-Zebub, the god of Ekron?" 2nd Kings 1:3.

Robert Ulrich, Chief Justice, Missouri Court of Appeals Western District, explained during the 1990(s): "We as Christian Americans are confronted with many issues reflecting that Christian principles are not standard in America today. Violent crime has risen 560% since 1960. Less than 1% of all Americans had used illegal drugs before 1960. By 1967, that number had risen to 17%. Today, 5,000 Americans will use an illegal drug for the first time."

"As a judge, I'm alarmed at the number of cases involving children who are sexually abused. I read recently that one in three girls and one in five boys are sexually assaulted before their 18th birthday. The teen suicide rate has tripled since 1960."

Chief Justice Ulrich continues, "Nationally, numerous allegations are asserted that the Chief Executive has engaged in a pattern of illicit sexual conduct, and what is particularly disturbing is that many pundits claim that, if it's true, it doesn't matter because the economy is doing well and it's a personal matter."

All this is to say that America is in moral decay and at best is on spiritual life support. Will America continue its plunge into apostasy?

"Christ and His work were always and will always be a stone of stumbling and rock of offence, a gin and a snare to many… And if one kind of stumbling-blocks are removed, it is to be expected that others will come. It is with Christ's works as it was with His parables; things that are difficult to men's dark minds are ordered of purpose, for the trial of their dispositions and spiritual sense; and that those of corrupt minds and of an unbelieving, perverse, caviling spirit, 'seeing might see and not understand'," Jonathan Edwards on Revival, page 133.

Remnant Within the Church

The spiritual gifts given by God to the Church carry serious stewardship responsibility. Ignoring both the responsibility to edify the Church, and the Great Commission for making disciples, are detrimental and ultimately destructive to any congregation of believers.

The admonition and exhortation for the Church from Scripture is return to God, repent of sin, and obey the Great Commission commanded by Jesus, "Go, therefore and make disciples of all the nations, baptizing them in the name of the Father and of the Son and of the Holy Spirit, teaching them to observe all things that I have commanded you; and lo, I am with you always, even to the end of the age." Matthew 28:19-20.

Speaking to the remnant in the Church, a promise and an exhortation are given from Scripture, "If My people who are called by My name will humble themselves, and pray and seek My face, and turn from their wicked ways, then I will hear from heaven, and will forgive their sin and heal their land," 2nd Chronicles 7:14.

Chapter 3

The Drift and Apathy Within the Evangelical Church

"Every citizen has a duty to learn more about the menace that threatens his future, his home, his children, the peace of the world -- and that is why I have written this book."

That was a statement from J. Edgar Hoover, former Director of the Federal Bureau of Investigation who authored "Masters of Deceit," 1958. Mr. Hoover was sounding an alarm from the threat of communism. After reading the book it seemed to me there ought to be an alarm sounded by the Church in America. "Flee from the wrath to come!" Matthew 3:7.

Most evangelical Pastors, Elders, and Deacons today would respond that this message must be for someone else. Wrong! It is for you, a leader and a member of the Church! Wake from your slumber! Do not think you have already fled to Christ while your own congregation and neighborhood is apathetic toward sin and apostasy. Death and hell are never satisfied!

Paul Settle warns, "The world, the flesh and the devil never cease trying to destroy the Church of Jesus Christ. The Church is in the world, and necessarily so, for this is where she must witness to Christ. But unfortunately, the world is also in the Church, tempting her to turn off the highways of biblical truth into detours of error and compromise," "To God all Praise and Glory," page 13.

"In the 1930(s) the Bible-believing Christians had stood together as liberalism came in to steal the Churches. Then at different speeds the liberals achieved their theft of the various denominations by gaining control of the power centers of the seminaries and the bureaucracies. At this point onward, Bible-believing Christians, instead of standing together, divided into two groups: those who held to the principle of the purity of the visible Church, and those who accepted and acted upon the concept of a pluralistic Church," "The Great Evangelical Disaster," Francis Schaeffer, page 74.

There is a distinct falling away, or apostasy, foretold in Scripture! There will be a rebellion against the Christian faith. A falling away will occur within the ranks of the members of the visible church. "Let no one deceive you by any means; for that day will not come unless the falling away comes first…" 2nd Thessalonians 2:3.

"When in many European countries today, countries which have known the gospel for centuries, people stay away from Church in droves – surely this is apostasy. When many so-called Christian leaders, both in Europe and America, deny cardinal teachings of the Bible like the bodily resurrection of Christ and still claim to be Christian theologians – surely this is apostasy. When preachers proclaim myths instead of facts, existentialist philosophy instead of Christian theology, humanism instead of the truth of the gospel - surely this is apostasy," "The Bible and the Future," Anthony A. Hoekema, page 154.

Warning and Exhortation

Jonathan Edwards exhorts and encourages the Church in America, "The devil has ever shown a mortal spite and hatred towards that holy book the Bible: he has done all in his power to extinguish that light; and to draw men off from it: he knows it to be that light by which his kingdom of darkness is to be overthrown... it is his constant plague. It is the main weapon which Michael uses in his war with him: it is the sword of the Spirit that pierces him and conquers him." "Jonathan Edwards on Revival," page 114.

The drift toward apostasy in America came with its affluence and its blessed abundance. Rather that thanking God for His bountiful gifts and abundant mercy, the Church went adrift. About forty years ago, Francis A/ Schaeffer asked the question in his book, "No Little People," page 176, "What then are we going to do with this Savior of the world?"

The more succinct question is what am I, or what are you, going to do with the Savior of the world?

The Church today with its liberal world-life view and its social politics is still preoccupied with things other than the Great Commission. The Church in America is now pathetically adrift!

"If you have much of the Spirit, decide to expect opposition both in and out of the Church. The leaders of the Church will probably fight you, which was true even for Christ. If you are far above their state of heart, other members will attack you, for anyone who lives a godly life in Christ Jesus must expect persecution. Elders and even the Pastor will fight against you if you are filled with the Spirit of God," "Lectures on Revival," Charles G. Finney, page 79.

Some estimates tell us less than 12% of Churches today financially support foreign missions. Even so, the majority of evangelical leaders in America will not actively participate in disciple making within their own hometowns!

The local Church typically does not consider authentic disciple making a priority! Though many Churches offer worthy Christian service opportunities, things are not as they appear! The Church in large measure has an agenda that appears to be a prescription for destruction. The wolves, having crept into positions of leadership in many Churches, are engaged more in marketing the Church than lifting up the name of Jesus, the propitiation for sin, the Son of God who satisfies the law and wrath of God.

The Apostle Paul warned the Elders at Ephesus, "For I know this, that after my departure savage wolves will come in among you, not sparing the flock. Also from among yourselves men will rise up, speaking perverse things, to draw away the disciples after themselves," Acts 20:29-30.

Paul Settle pleads against liberalism, "Theological liberalism scorches the ecclesiastical landscape, turning it into a desert; devoid of the Spirit, it dries up the springs of spiritual nurture; wanting the Word, it withers the soul," "To God all Power and Glory," page 28.

"Be careful not to complain about blunt, pointed preaching, especially if it seems directed at you. Churches forget that a minister is responsible only to God. They want their pastor's sermons to never criticize them. If he bears down and exposes the sins prevailing in the Church, they cry, 'Too personal!' and rebel against the truth," "Lectures on Revival," Charles G. Finney, page 148.

Conforming to the World

As recent as Saturday, June 5, 2010, a Birmingham, Alabama news article reported that a particular denominational conference was held. It was announced that a certain evangelical denomination would close the doors to 12 of its churches in Alabama. The reason for this action is membership has declined. This, of course, is but a miniscule picture of the Church in the United States. During the last two decades, thousands of evangelical Churches in America closed their doors permanently! Cobwebs and dust took over where the gospel of our Lord ceased to be preached and disciple making was ignored. "…Liberals did not believe in the necessity of regeneration and conversion for people to become Christians; they believed that all men would somehow be saved," <u>"To God all Power and Glory,"</u> Paul Settle, page 30.

A Bishop in this aforementioned news article pointed out, "Pastors will receive training and coaching on Church growth and effective leadership techniques." Like most Churches of our day, the focus of the news article is on revitalization efforts and strategies. No word was reported concerning the essentials of the gospel of Jesus Christ. No word was spoken of the promise that if Jesus is proclaimed, then the Holy Spirit will draw all men to the Savior. Rather, the Bishop explained, "If we just set the goals and the numbers, God will tell them [Pastors] how to do it."

Sadly, this is what most Churches did in Europe in decades past. The Bishop seems to imply, we set the numbers, and God will comply. Would you believe that some Christians think it is inappropriate to share Christ with people of other faiths?

Randy Alcorn explains, "Thirty years ago, many people chose churches based on whether the Church believed and taught the truth. Today, many choose Churches based on whether the Church makes them feel comfortable. If a Church tells the truth, it will gain some people but loose others." "Unfortunately, many nonbelievers know only two kinds of Christians: those who speak the truth without grace and those who are very nice but never share the truth," <u>The Grace and Truth Paradox,</u> pages 76-77.

Have you, Church leader, observed spiritual weakness in your Church members who neither witness nor desire to appropriate the "means of grace" for their witness? Prayer, Bible, Worship, Fellowship, and Witness are unquestionably the means of grace used in disciple making.

It appears the last things evangelicals want to exercise are a ready witness or share the gospel in their neighborhood. Why? Most of them have not been trained! They were not trained as witnesses or disciples, and therefore they did not become disciple makers.

Attempting to Serve Two Masters

Those of us who have a witness and do share the gospel often times are quite weak in the follow-up element of ministry. The follow up in the disciple-making ministry is thought to be mostly shallow or the weakest element in evangelistic outreach. We stop short in our responsibility.

Rather than invest in the new convert with our time and personal attention, we miss the opportunity to impart spiritual lessons that lead to maturity. We miss the opportunity to mentor and consequently we de-emphasize the importance of discipleship.

If you use the Evangelism Explosion guidelines, or the Roman Road gospel presentation, the Four Spiritual Laws, the Navigators' presentation, or some other biblical approach, do not leave the new born to find his or her own way thereafter. Follow up with the new convert, e.g., encouraging them to join a Bible study, is crucial for them to achieve maturity. The love of God is the motivator and your joy in the Lord is its own reward.

The lack of a thoroughgoing commitment to disciple making impacts the way prospective members are accepted into the church. Rather than asking the prospective member, what is it you believe about Christ? And what has Christ specifically done for you? Prospective members are merely asked to give assent to a list of items read to them in a general and less than personal way.

It should be noted here that many Churches in America have ordained Teaching Elders who deny fundamental biblical doctrines. "Controversies began to rage about the doctrines of the nature and extent of the inspiration of the Holy Scriptures, the Virgin Birth of Christ, His bodily resurrection and His substitutionary atonement," "To God All Praise and Glory," Paul Settle, page 15.

The writer of Hebrews admonishes and exhorts the Church, "For it is impossible for those who were once enlightened, and have tasted the heavenly gift, and have become partakers of the Holy Spirit, and have tasted the good word of God and the powers of the age to come, if they fall away, to renew them again to repentance, since they crucify again for themselves the Son of God and put Him to an open shame," Hebrews 6:4-6. Note that those who were "enlightened" were not described by the Apostle as the elect. Nor are they identified as being converted or justified. There are some in leadership within the Church that function as if they are in the corporate world and not as soldiers of the cross. Are these Church leaders enlightened or are they actually the elect?

Numerous Church leaders apparently do not bear fruit themselves, nor are they willing to devote themselves to receiving training first as a disciple. These leaders may participate in the activities of the Church routinely. They might have been circumcised, baptized, evangelized, enjoy the fellowship of believers, and serve on several committees.

However, if any leader actually becomes a disciple, then he is exposed to a learning responsibility, a training commitment, and accountability that will cause a man to examine himself. There is a commitment to obedience, participation in, and perseverance to authentic way-of-life ministry. It is a superb opportunity for the Church leader to be changed, to grow, and to glorify God. "No servant can serve two masters; for either he will hate the one and love the other, or else he will be loyal to the one and despise the other. You cannot serve God and mammon," Luke 16:13.

Need for Self Examination

Discipleship has to do with much self-examination in light of the Word. A disciple-making ministry challenges the Church leader by bringing him into a closer relationship with the Lord. It is a relationship and an awareness that has more depth, and height, and breadth than one has ever experienced.

There are other things brought to bear, things that have not entered the heart or mind of the committed disciple. The disciple maker, due to a more earnest prayer life, greater participation in worship, and Bible study, finds that self-examination becomes necessary. "For the word of God is living and powerful, sharper than any two-edged sword, piercing even to the division of soul and spirit, and of joints and marrow, and is a discerner of the thoughts and intents of the heart," Hebrews 4:12.

"Therefore, if anyone is in Christ, he is a new creation; old things have passed away; behold, all things have become new," 2nd Corinthians 5:17.

We are to be made holy as we depend upon God who completes the work that He began in us. "Just as He chose us in Him before the foundation of the world, that we should be holy and without blame before Him in love, having predestined us to adoption as sons by Jesus Christ to Himself, according to the good pleasure of His will, to the praise of the glory of His grace, by which He made us accepted in the Beloved," Ephesians 1:4-6.

As a disciple, the opportunity to serve the Lord is at hand in ways not experienced before. The disciple has tasted of the Lord and nothing else will ever satisfy him. The disciple maker has a greater sense of awareness and sees more and more opportunities to winsomely engage others concerning the gospel. He or she also becomes more sensitive to the leading of the Holy Spirit. There is unspeakable joy that human words cannot describe.

It ascribes glory to Almighty God for His love, faithfulness, and holy purpose.

Chapter 4

Knowledge Without Love

A few years ago, our grandson Will Crain came home
from Oak Mountain Classical School one afternoon
and began to quote his memory work from Psalm 139.
As he quoted verse 6, it especially drew my heart
toward the Lord, "Such knowledge is too wonderful for
me; it is high, I cannot attain unto it."

I know the Lord is perfect, holy, and never changes.
My limited knowledge of the Lord reminds me of my
fallen nature and my selfish tendencies. Many years ago
I followed after those things offered by the world.
Lessons learned came very hard. My burden of sin and
guilt was more than one could bear. As a seventeen-
year-old, the thought of tomorrow held great fear and
uncertainty for me.

Bert Anderson, [a.k.a. "B.I."] our Pastor at Alta Woods
Presbyterian Church, Jackson, Mississippi explained to
me, one-on-one, that, "Jesus came to seek and to save

that which was lost," Luke 19:10. If that was the qualification, then it described me to a tee! What wondrous hope, to be reconciled to God in Jesus! Bert explained it was his only hope as well. What a wonderful gift from God! It is a gift that certainly was not earned or deserved by me.

Nevertheless, the life that I now live, I live by the faith of the Son of God, who died and gave Himself a ransom for me. I am in full agreement with the Psalmist, "Such knowledge is too wonderful for me; it is high, I cannot attain unto it."

A man, who was blind from birth, as described in the New Testament, explained after an encounter with Jesus of Nazareth, "…Whether He is a sinner or not I do not know. One thing I know: that though I was blind, now I see," John 9:25. What more can I say to you dear reader, except that Jesus saves!

My own salvation was not dependent upon me, or my limited and shallow intellect, utter lack of talent, diminutive stature, non-existent social status, invisible affluence, or some imagined political connection. It is by grace alone, by faith alone, in Jesus Christ alone that anyone is reconciled to God and adopted into the family of God.

You may inquire, "How can anyone conceal such great news?" The answer is that I cannot. The light so graciously given comes with a very high stewardship responsibility. It speaks of the most profound message of Scripture, "Jesus loves me!" That message was articulated back in 1860 by Anna B. Warner, living on

Martyr's Island in the Hudson estuary, who penned the hymn, "Jesus Loves Me."

Absence of Godly Love in the Church

Standing in sharp contrast to this message is the weak testimony of many in Church leadership in America today. All this is to say, if a Pastor, or leader in the Church has academic knowledge concerning Jesus, but lacks the love of Jesus that overflows from grace given by the Holy Spirit toward sinners, his ministry is, very sadly, in vain.

Absent Godly love, no one calling himself Senior Pastor, Bishop, Elder, or Deacon, will come close to being directly involved in a disciple-making ministry. They will be cleverly determined to avoid that responsibility. They deserve sound rebuke for neglecting their God-given commission and should be challenged by their peers!

The necessity for mature discipleship leaders, and a disciple-making ministry, will not make the list of strategic ministry essentials for many Pastors. Hence, cobwebs, empty pews and disappointment will one day replace their congregation, absent divine intervention. This is the legacy of disobedient Church leadership in Europe. The Church in England, France, etc. abdicated from its disciple-making responsibilities.

Not surprisingly, many Churches in America will have to close their doors. Membership decline, to some degree, will ultimately inspire some Church leaders, in desperation, to begin what they call "outreach." But, apart from Jesus and His gospel, they can do nothing.

Occasionally, a Church-appointed search committee will seek a Senior Pastor with substantial academic degrees who may pontificate through grandiose oratory. But his ministry may lack God–given power especially if there is an absence of love for Jesus, His Church, and for the lost; academic degrees and oratory notwithstanding. That being the case, there is no unction! That ministry is not Spirit-led. Apart from God, who is love, that Pastor can do nothing! "God is love," 1st John 4:8b.

Jesus came to seek and to save that which is lost! There is limited conviction that goes beyond the pulpit when love is absent. Stories and amusement for the congregation serve as a substitute or filler. So-called contemporary music, most of which is lacking in biblical substance, is sometimes incorporated into the worship service. It is thought to attract some folks for a time, especially younger folks! And it does, for a time. Many want to feel good about their Church, their sense of community, their closed circle of friends while Rome burns, or in this case Rome is the United States of America.

Membership outreach, marketing programs, accelerated community appeal, and even evangelism classes, while neglecting the responsibility for the Great Commission, generally results in temporary feel-good ministry. Therefore, a Church's ministry is purposely, defiantly, and seriously limited.

Worldly Solutions Amiss

Where is the love that ought to be demonstrated, in our cities, by Spirit–lead Church leadership? Pastor Alistair Begg, preaching about the duty of the Church pointed out, "It is not the mission of the Church to find new and interesting ideas to make the Church grow, but to go on preaching the same fundamental truths which she has always proclaimed... At every period in the history of the Church the greatest sin of the Church and the one that causes the greatest distress is that she withholds the gospel from the world and from herself. She does not know the reason for her own existence and consequently has no real message for the present situation."

Liberalism and Progressivism is determined to employ worldly solutions to achieve its goals. "Further, liberal leaders made it clear that ministers and members of the Church who did not agree were not only out of step, but out of bounds. Dissenters were scorned, called reactionary, disloyal and worse, systematically excluded from denominational committees..." "To God All Praise and Glory," Paul Settle, page 21.

Writing to the Church at Corinth, Paul explained, "Though I speak with the tongues of men and of angles, but have not love, I have become sounding brass or a clanging symbol. And though I have the gift of prophecy, and understand all mysteries and all knowledge and though I have all faith, so that I could remove mountains, but have not love, I am nothing. And though I bestow all my goods to feed the poor, and though I give my body to be burned, but have not love, it profits me nothing. ... And now abide faith, hope, and love, these three; but the greatest of these is love," 1 Cor. 13:1-3 & 13.

All of this is to say that knowledge, contemporary music, and sense of community without love cannot be expected to bear fruit. "By this all will know that you are my disciples, if you have love for one another," John 13:35.

Without Me, You Can Do Nothing

Several years ago Francis Schaeffer admonished numerous worldly Churches by pointing out, "And let us understand that to accommodate the world spirit about us in our age is nothing less than the most gross form of worldliness in the proper definition of that word. And with this proper definition of worldliness, we must say with tears that, with exceptions, the evangelical Church is worldly and not faithful to the living Christ," "The Great Evangelical Disaster," Francis Schaeffer, page 38.

Without discipleship and disciple makers, fruit bearing will be sparse, if at all existent! The gospel of Jesus Christ is the power of God unto Salvation to everyone who believes in Jesus and His completed work for sinners by His shed blood on the cross. "...Without shedding of blood there is no remission [of sin]," Hebrews 9:22.

Church leadership must be wholly dependent on the abiding principle. "I am the Vine, you are the branches. He who abides in Me, and I in him, bears much fruit;

for without Me you can do nothing. If anyone does not abide in Me, he is cast out as a branch and is withered; and they gather them and throw them into the fire, and they are burned. If you abide in Me, and My words abide in you, you will ask what you desire, and it shall be done for you. By this My Father is glorified, that you bear much fruit; so you will be My Disciples," John 15:5-8.

Chapter 5

Ignoring the Call
to Disciple making

Were you and I, dear reader, looking for a church home, there would certainly be the essentials that we could require before joining any congregation. We, as evangelicals, would demand that the Church must be a congregation of believers that held to the Bible as the inspired word of God, infallible, God – breathed, without error, the only infallible rule of faith and practice.

We would insist on a biblical form of church government that is representative, transparent, and accountable. A Church of our choosing must preach the word of God, the gospel of Jesus, in and out of season; adhere to the Westminster Confession and the Apostle's Creed, and properly administer the Sacraments of Baptism and Communion instituted by Jesus.

We would expect there to be a proper administration of Church discipline, something that is sorely lacking in the Church today, or abused to perpetuate power. "It is a mournful fact that many churches refuse to take sin seriously... it would be difficult to show another area of Christian life which is more commonly ignored by the modern evangelical Church than Church discipline," "Biblical Church Discipline," Daniel E. Wray, page 1.

We would anticipate the Church of our choosing to support a generous ministry for the benefit of widows and the fatherless. It would be a place of warm welcome to every stranger.

We would desire, want, and pray for a Church with a heart and budget for missions, both foreign and domestic. Equally important, we should require the leadership in the Church, without exception, to be directly involved in intentional discipleship and disciple making themselves, otherwise, if not disciples by example, then they are but hypocrites.

Spirit-led fruit bearing by Church leadership is more than good. It is essential to the testimony and propagation of the Church in an increasingly secular culture. The proclamation of the gospel by Church officers is the acid test of commitment within the government of the Church itself. It is the manifest evidence of loving and serving the only living and ruling Lord, Jesus Christ.

Whom Shall I Send?

An Elder should be apt to teach! Teaching by example through disciple making is a concrete way to incentivize the prayer ministry. Disciple making is prescribed from Scripture as the means to reach your Jerusalem and other nations.

Alarmingly, most Church leaders don't buy into the example given by Isaiah with respect to the office of a disciple-messenger. "Also I heard the voice of the Lord, saying: Whom shall I send, and who will go for Us? Then I said, 'Here am I! Send me'," Isaiah 6:8. When Church leaders are asked to participate in a disciple-making ministry, the excuse often given by many is, "I don't have the gift of evangelism!"

Sadly, I am convinced it is easier, in most Churches, to send a missionary to a foreign country on the opposite end of the earth than it is to ask a Pastor, Elder, or Deacon to winsomely greet a stranger on the street, or an occasional church visitor, and ask for permission to share their testimony and the gospel of Jesus.

Study, Then Work

If you, however, are a Church leader who is a disciple and a disciple maker, then disregard this observation of most leaders I have met. You are part of a company of rare, but obedient disciples.

Certainly, there is a degree of empathy here for Church leadership. About 30 years ago,

I was challenged to actively participate in a discipleship ministry and subsequently intentional disciple making. I was not at all comfortable walking up to a stranger and sharing the gospel.

Therefore, I did what I estimate 97% plus of all evangelicals do. I kept quiet. After all, there was no risk in keeping quiet. There certainly was not going to be any rejection of the gospel or of me personally.

But that behavior or attitude of heart is sin. It is completely ignoring my responsibility for the Great Commission that is given to each person who names the name of Jesus. If we are ashamed of Him, then He has reason to be ashamed of us before the Father. "For whoever is ashamed of Me and My words in this adulterous and sinful generation, of him the Son of Man also will be ashamed when He comes in the glory of His Father with the holy angles," Mark 8:38.

We are not required to save a certain number of souls, though one who is a soul-winner is a wise person according to Scripture. "The fruit of righteousness is a tree of life, and he who wins souls is wise," Proverbs 11:30. We are, however, required to study the word and to have a reason for the faith that lies within us. "Be diligent to present yourself approved to God, a worker who does not need to be ashamed, rightly dividing the word of truth," 2nd Timothy 2:15.

It is the Holy Spirit who brings to remembrance all that is needful during our times of witnessing. The Apostle Paul reminds us to be a Jew to the Jew and to be a Greek to the Greek. Jesus explained, "Do not worry about how or what you should speak. For it will be given to you in that hour what you should speak; for it is not you who speak, but the Spirit of your Father who speaks in you," Matthew 10:19. Do not be an offense to any man. Reason together. If any man rejects the gospel of Jesus, then he rejects the One who sent us. We are to quietly excuse ourselves, shake the dust from our sandals, and continue on our journey

Hearing His Voice

Dear reader, if you are a Christian, then test the resources of God. F. B. Meyer, 1847-1929, a Baptist Pastor from England, once explained, "We never test the resources of God until we attempt the impossible!" Jesus explained, "Do not be concerned for what you will say. I will put my words in your mouth," [paraphrased]. That has been the experience of multitudes of Christian witnesses for two-thousand years. "Therefore settle it in your hearts not to meditate beforehand on what you will answer; for I will give you a mouth and wisdom which all your adversaries will not be able to contradict or resist," Luke 21:14-15.

"For you see your calling, brethren, that not many wise according to the flesh, not many mighty, not many noble are called," 1st Corinthians 1:26. But God calls each one He has saved in Jesus Christ to be His witnesses. "Let your light so shine before men, that they may see your good works and glorify your Father in heaven," Matthew 5:16. "My sheep hear My voice, and I know them, and they follow Me," John 10:27.

Do you hear His voice, dear Reader? Would you be a faithful under shepherd and disciple maker in your Church? Ask God for His Spirit. He freely gives grace to all those who come to Him in repentance of sin and faith in Jesus.

Today is the day of salvation! "For with the heart one believes unto righteousness, and with the mouth confession is made unto salvation," Romans 10:10. Come to our Lord Jesus today and be reconciled to God!

Chapter 6

Measure of a Healthy Church

"As iron sharpens iron, so a man sharpens the countenance of his friend," Proverbs 27:17. All of us need oversight, accountability, exhortation and encouragement. This is certainly true for the local Church. Introspection and evaluation of ministry, at least annually, is imperative. It especially applies in the disciple-making ministry.

Disciple making is a training, equipping, accountability, and deployment ministry! It is where the local church member winsomely comes into contact with the community at large, one person at-a-time, face-to-face. Each Church member ought to be equipped by his or her leadership for Spirit-led ministry. "... Do not sorrow, for the joy of the Lord is your strength," Nehemiah 8:10b.

Missionaries, as you know, are typically sent into Judea, Samaria, and the uttermost parts of the world.

But equally, if not more importantly, is the deployment of Church members into their own Jerusalem! The goal, in part, is to keep the local Church strong, battle-ready, and to perpetuate disciple making for future generations in obedience to the Great Commission.

Reaching your city, your Jerusalem, with the gospel is the responsibility of the local Church member, not some Church staff employee. Reaching your neighbor with the gospel is neither the responsibility of a guest speaker, nor that of an entertainment group, nor is it a thing that happens without lay people from the congregation being involved.

The disciple-making ministry responsibility falls squarely on the shoulders of Church Pastors and officers to "Go!" Not to stay in the church! Disciple making is done, in large part, outside of the local Church building by and through the examples demonstrated by authentic leadership to its membership.

Disciple Development

Disciples must be taken outside of the Church and into the community to pray for and watch the example of a disciple maker. No excuse is acceptable otherwise! We, the Church members, are to be salt and light in our own town and neighborhoods.

Each adult Church member's testimony, along with the light of the gospel, will be kept under a bushel if that person is not thoroughly equipped, deployed, and held accountable. They should be given the opportunity to participate with their leadership in an in-home visitation ministry. The discipleship ministry must be prayer supported and intentionally planned! Both the disciples and the disciple makers must be armed with prayer and supported by specific, designated, prayer warriors prior to deployment. Otherwise, without prayer, deployment is in vain. "That which is born of the flesh is flesh, and that which is born of the Spirit is spirit," John 3:6. The soldiers of the cross, the disciples and the disciple makers, must be thoughtful, prayerful, and well-practiced in their personal testimony and well-schooled in the gospel. After one full semester of training, which includes being led by a disciple maker, the trainee or disciple is expected to function as an acting disciple maker during the second semester. After two full semesters, one as a disciple and the second as an acting disciple maker, he or she is ready to be certified competent, following a written and an oral examination. Ministry structure and training is outlined in chapter 13.

Given the expectations of a disciple-making ministry, how might we measure progress within the local church? What are some of the visible benchmarks of progress that we may use for examining our own church in light of our responsibility to make disciples?

The Imperative, Follow Me

A reasonable place to begin is to look at the size of your own church. How many members do you have? What does the membership trend look like over the past year, two years, and five years? Is membership increasing or decreasing? Do you know why?

What percent of your members are at Church on a typical Sunday? What percent of your members are in Sunday school each week? How many Bible studies or catechism classes do our Pastors, Elders, and Deacons lead during the week? What percent of our members attend these classes? Would you care to examine the details and compare them to a healthy Church? What are reasonable expectations for disciple making by your Church leadership in its battle against an overwhelming secular culture?

Does this approach look like the typical marketing analysis process? Perhaps, but we have not begun the critique of our commitment and performance as disciple makers. We have only begun to look at the obvious.

Generally, it ought to be a requirement in the local Church for all Ruling Elders and Senior Deacons to teach Bible or catechism during the week in addition to Sundays. It is especially important that this expectation be articulated by Church leadership and emulated by all Pastors. If any leader is not 'apt to teach' or will not teach, then encourage him to resign immediately!

If in fact the Pastors and other leaders do not participate in Bible teaching outside of Sunday, there is already a hole in the Church's boat! Why would you be surprised if your boat, the local Church, sank in one generation and the Church had to close its doors forever?

Right from the start, Church leadership must of necessity follow the example set by our Lord. Jesus led

His disciples in active ministry for three years! He taught them how to pray. He took them everywhere! They went into their society, into the synagogue, into the market place, into the countryside, into the mountains, into the sea, into the homes of sinners, and on mission trips. Jesus said, "… Follow me and I will make you fishers of men," Matthew 4:19. Jesus did not remain inside the synagogue waiting for visitors!

Just prior to His Ascension, Jesus' last command to His disciples was given, "Go therefore and make disciples of all the nations," Matthew 28:19.

Examine Your Ministry

Discipleship implies that you graduate from novice [disciple] to disciple-maker. That will not be accomplished by staying inside the walls of the Church. "And the things that you [Timothy] have heard from me [Paul] among many witnesses, commit these to faithful men who will be able to teach others also. No one engaged in warfare entangles himself with the affairs of this life, that he may please him who enlisted him as a soldier," 2nd Timothy 2:2,4.

Does your Church leadership appear on Sunday and disappear for the rest of the week? If they do, what is wrong with this picture? There is an old saying that a fish rots from the head downward. Perhaps that is true. But if a Church does not have biblical leadership, it is in error. Leadership and obedience to the Great Commission go hand-in-hand and are best accomplished by example, not by dictum!

How many visitors from the local community do you have in Church on Sunday?
How many visitors come to Sunday school and Bible study classes during the week?
Is it known? Is it published? Are all of these visitors called on at home by someone in leadership soon after their first visit?

Does the first-time local visitor get to hear a personal testimony and the gospel, in their home, within a week to 10 days after their first visit to your Church? Do you, dear reader, understand the implications of this line of questioning?

Ministry Impact Measurement

We will begin to bring our message closer to the point. How many of your Church members have had discipleship training for at least two school semesters during the course of a year? How many of those completing the training are 'certified competent' to train others in disciple making?

We should expect that all those in leadership positions within the Church, including the Senior Pastor, be 'certified competent' only after participating in two disciple-making semesters. Thereafter, all men in Church leadership should routinely serve in the disciple-making ministry six-months out of every year through a planned visitation ministry within their own town.

Discipleship ministry service is, very importantly, relational. It may be experienced in various capacities, e.g., teacher of a discipleship curriculum, leader and trainer of discipleship for in-home visitation, discipleship apologetics training, discipleship prayer ministry, scheduling of contacts for in-home visits to members, visitors, and strangers; and also discipleship recruitment, and support services in music, hospitality, etc. All of these job descriptions are outlined in chapter thirteen.

Here are some of the primary areas to measure progress in the ministry of discipleship and disciple making: How many adult professions of faith did we have during the last year, two years, and five years? Children, whose parents are not Church members, but who are making a profession of faith for the first time, ought to be counted as a separate figure.

How many first-time adult baptisms did our Church have during the last year, two years and five years? Children, whose parents are not Church members, but who are being baptized for the first time, ought to be counted as a separate figure.

Adult professions of faith and first-time adult baptisms in the Church are quite significant. They generally represent a visible result of a fruit-bearing, disciple-making ministry. The impact of the gospel message commonly results in the Holy Spirit drawing some men into the kingdom of God and often into the local Church.

Intentional Disciple Making

All of this means, the discipleship and disciple-making ministry must be organized and implemented by the senior Church leadership. It must be planned, intentional, thoughtful, and scheduled. In other words, it is an act of obedience, motivated by gratitude, and it is a purposeful response to the love and command of God.

It is leadership's response to a command from our Lord! It takes the gospel of Jesus Christ into the local community. It glorifies God, who alone is worthy. "The Lord is... not willing that any should perish but that all should come to repentance," 2 Peter 3:9.

Our Lord has determined discipleship to be an important means to accomplish His holy will. Why, then, is the majority of Church leadership not in pursuit of that which will bring the membership to greater maturity through its obedience to God?

Are we living in an age when men in Church leadership will not endure sound doctrine? This is at the heart of our argument, with respect to contemporary Church leadership, for the crisis of disobedience in the Evangelical Church.

"For the time will come when they will not endure sound doctrine, but according to their own desires, because they have itching ears, they will heap up for themselves teachers; and they will turn their ears away from the truth, and be turned aside to fables. But you be watchful in all things, endure afflictions, do the work of an evangelist, fulfill your ministry," 2nd Timothy 4:3-5.

The biblical solution for bringing your membership into maturity is found in intentional, prayerful, studied, accountable, and disciplined discipleship. The Senior Pastor must lead the discipleship and disciple-making ministry. The attitude of heart, in all humility, requires first love to God, then to love our neighbor as ourselves. The United States of America is in need of the testimony of the local Church.

What is that still small voice saying to you, dear reader, with respect to the Great Commission? Make yourself available, and God can make you useable.

The Lord is no respecter of persons. "For there is no partiality with God," Romans 2:11.

"Then Peter opened his mouth and said: "In truth I perceive that God shows not partiality," Acts 10:34.

Chapter 7

Easy way out, Evangelism without Discipleship

My purpose is not to judge the Church, but to create awareness, and then to exhort and encourage you, the Christian man or woman, to accept your God-given Commission, Church leadership notwithstanding. Know what your leadership is doing with respect to the Great Commission in your Jerusalem. "… The harvest truly is plentiful, but the laborers are few. Therefore pray the Lord of the harvest to send out laborers into His harvest," Matthew 9:37-38.

My observations of the Church are certainly not error-free. I am convinced; nevertheless, there is widespread decay in terms of exceedingly progressive Church leadership. All too common we find local Churches that have a feel-good, market-driven message, or a name-it-and-claim-it, or otherwise diluted ministry. Christ and Him crucified for sinners is no longer central to their message! There are also some in Church leadership today in the United States who use the pulpit to spread the message of liberation theology, which is Marxism in Christian terms. There are also other churches that have evolved primarily for social purposes. Both are in serious error.

I have also observed as a Church member, the less than urgent priority of many in leadership as it relates to their active participation in disciple making. They avoid teaching their members how to develop their own Christian testimony and how to share the gospel. Certainly, there are exceptions, but I speak, with much grief, concerning the majority in leadership across evangelical denominations.

Don't miss this point. Jesus is the biblical example for discipleship and disciple making!

I've explained on occasion, perhaps poorly, to those whom I have trained as a disciple, that if God can use Balaam's donkey to deliver a message, then He can use the man or woman who makes themselves available to Him. See Numbers 22:28-30. The Lord uses the man or woman who trusts Him for the opportunity to deliver a timely gospel message in due season.

Do you remember when someone, in Christian love, shared the gospel with you? Do you recall your first understanding of the gospel's significance to you personally? You, at that time, realized the gospel is the very best news you ever heard! In all probability, the message delivered to you was delivered by a layperson within the local church and not a Pastor. Are you surprised?

Discipleship in Action

One such organization of laypersons is the Gideons. They are made up of all volunteers. The Gideons are not paid or reimbursed for their expenses. They count it a high privilege to deliver the layman's ministry message to local Evangelical Church congregations. The Gideon ministry to date, has given, free-of-charge, over 1.2 billion Bibles, in 89 different languages, to people all over the world.

There are, at this writing, about 150,000 Gideon workers in 175 countries and there is not a Pastor in the bunch! They are laymen! Presently, along with the Gideon women's auxiliary, their goal is to deliver, with their own testimonies, no less than 100,000,000 Bibles annually, worldwide, by the year 2020.

The Gideon ministry is a good example of how a professional, or businessman, as a member of an evangelical Church in good standing, may become involved in discipleship and ultimately disciple making in their Jerusalem. Nevertheless, some in Church leadership are opposed to it for any number of reasons. Some Church leaders erroneously regard the Gideon ministry as a competing rather than complementary ministry. It is a ministry for laymen to reach their community with their testimony and the word of God. One hundred percent of the donations given to the Gideon ministry are applied to the printing and distribution of the King James New Testament Bible, and it includes Psalms and Proverbs from the Old Testament. The Gideons themselves pay for the operational overhead of this ministry through their dues and donations. That is a pretty good track record for a lay-ministry!

Are you aware, though Jesus is the superlative of everything good you can say about Him, there is today a huge number of Church congregations in the United States that no longer welcome Gideon representatives to speak or give their testimony concerning Jesus?

More Caught than Taught

Many Churches, in recent decades, have succumbed to a "softer evangelism." They may generally offer a Sunday school evangelism class that teaches the Roman Road presentation, The Four Spiritual Laws, the Navigators Presentation or some variation on the gospel message.

Classes that teach evangelism are laudable. But there is a strategic, significant failure when personal in-home visitation or some form of deployment and accountability process is omitted in training the laity. In-home visitation is essential!

In-home visitation gives the novice disciple an opportunity to observe their disciple maker [trainer]. They observe, first hand, how to winsomely engage others and how to gain permission for presenting their testimony and the gospel.

Visitation, or deployment, is at the heart of disciple making. It provides the novice disciple an opportunity to gain confidence, and opportunities to critique their trainer after each visit and to ask questions.

The experience of multiple in-home visitation opportunities builds confidence for the novice disciple and it creates an awareness of the value of one's own worth and significance in ministry before God.

It is through visitation experience, relational contacts, and gradual participation in testimony and gospel presentations that fundamental equipping is accomplished for the novice disciple. It enables the disciple to grow and then to ultimately become a disciple maker. Disciple makers generally agree discipleship is, "More caught than taught." Also, inherent in the equipping process is a greater awareness of God's presence as we are obedient to His commands.

Years ago it was common for most Pastors and Church leadership to visit, at least once a year, in the home of each Church member. Most of that is lost today! Excuses are manifold! Relationships between Church leadership and the laity have become thin at best, or altogether superficial for the worst.

Missing the Mark

The cults, however, are quick to pick up the slack while evangelical leadership is negligent concerning their responsibility to visit local neighborhoods, their congregation, and visitors. In short, evangelical leadership appears to be asleep.

The Mormons, on the other hand, are famous for their dedication to visitation and thereby attract those who are looking for something to believe concerning God and truth. Mormonism, if you haven't noticed, is the fastest growing cult in America and it is growing while the evangelical Church is shrinking!

Jehovah's Witnesses and Seventh Day Adventists also employ visitation as a means for growing their numbers because the evangelicals have apparently abdicated their responsibility for in-home visitation.

Easy Way Out

The easy way out for contemporary Church leadership is to avoid the in-home visit. They avoid asking the Church member and the local visitor if a 3-person team may visit him or her for fifteen minutes sometime next week, in the evening, or at some other convenient time.

If leadership doesn't ask for permission to visit, then they don't have to go into someone's home. They can also avoid asking about those embarrassing prayer requests.

The easy way out for Church leadership is to have someone in the Church teach a class on evangelism without requiring accountability, deployment, or authentic disciple making! It deflects responsibility. It is a much-used routine that avoids acting on the command given by our Lord to "Go!" It is a routine that keeps the leadership inside the Church walls and comfortable in their own environment.

Most men in Church leadership positions today keep the light, which was given to the Church in the United States in decades past, under a bushel. Consequently, their example, testimony, and sharing of the gospel seems non-existent outside of the Church building to a large extent.

Chapter 8

Apart From Me,
Ye Can Do Nothing

Kennedy Smartt, in his book, explains, "Life in the Spirit begins with regeneration... Assurance of salvation is not based on any experience, but on the Word of God that promises eternal life to all who believe. This assurance is to be cultivated by the continual use of the means of grace," "I Am Reminded," page 222.

The means of grace in the Church is generally understood to be prayer, Bible study, worship, fellowship and witness. Would you, dear reader, dare to guess which area or element is typically the least appropriated and practiced in the Church in the United States today? The correct answer is witness!

Witness is built upon the other four elements in the means of grace. Our witness and our fruit bearing is a result from being filled by and walking in the Spirit. "The dominion of Christ in our lives occurs when we are led willingly by the Word through which the Spirit works," Kennedy Smartt," "I Am Reminded," page 222.

The Spirit brings all things to remembrance that we are to speak as we witness to others. "But the Helper, the Holy Spirit, whom the Father will send in My name, He will teach you all things, and bring to your remembrance all things that I said to you," John 14:26.

The Spirit enables the shy, the unskilled, the humble, the ordinary man, woman, and child, to speak in love and with exceptional boldness. Again, relying on the Spirit and not any special talent is essential. Jesus explained, "I am the vine, you are the branches. He who abides in Me, and I in him, bears much fruit; for without Me you can do nothing," John 15:5.

Spiritual gifts are to be used for the edification of the Church. We are all exhorted in Scripture to be ready to give an answer for the faith that lies within us. Do you profess to be a Christian? If yes, then you have a personal testimony. Your testimony is what has been revealed to you by the Spirit from the Word of God. Who is Jesus specifically? What has he done for you personally? And what is your life like now that you are His?

Answering these questions is the basis for a good testimony. It is important to be able to articulate your thoughts in a coherent manner concerning your witness or testimony. Generally, a one or two-minute monologue, practiced or written on a single sheet of paper, will be more than sufficient. That exercise will help you build your own testimony. No one else has your unique testimony. You have a personal relationship with the Master and it is your testimony.

Quite naturally, men, women and children do not generally see the necessity for the development of their testimony without giving thought to what will happen to others who do not repent of sin and believe in the Lord. Understanding the consequences of what will happen to others, apart from Jesus, should be sufficient motivation for all Christians to proclaim His gospel. Do we love our neighbor as much as ourselves?

Love and Communication

Most Church leaders in America avoid enlisting their members for discipleship training. They do not demonstrate how to develop a personal Christian testimony. Neither do they lead members into the local community to articulate and demonstrate how it is done.

They do not, for the most part, disciple their members in the area of witnessing and gospel sharing. Therefore, they are not developing the next generation of disciple makers. Consequently, Church leadership is negligent in taking the spiritual battle into their town, which is their Jerusalem

Why will the leadership in our Churches not commit to disciple making? The answer is because it first requires one to humble themselves in obedience and then to become a disciple who is not ashamed of Jesus. It requires sacrificial preparation. It is a life-long commitment to follow the Lord.

Discipleship affords a first-hand opportunity to experience and to somewhat understand the reality of all manner of spiritual opposition. Much of that opposition comes from those with a liberal or progressive persuasion. That opposition today, in large measure, is within the leadership of the Church itself!

Discipleship requires confrontation of our own sin, our own propensity to disobedience. Again, "No one can serve two masters; for either he will hate the one and love the other, or else he will be loyal to the one and despise the other. You cannot serve God and mammon," Matthew 6:24. The reality is that we have a momentary opportunity during our brief lives to serve a faithful Master who has promised to go with us, before us, and to use us in His glorious purpose.

"In words and practice the Church must also, as a corporate body, show that it takes holiness and love, and love and communication seriously. And how can it do this unless it consciously practices holiness and love, and love and communication, both toward those inside the Church group and those Christians outside the group? If the church... as a corporate body does not consciously seek freedom from the bonds of sin, and freedom from the results of the bonds of sin, on the basis of the finished work of Christ in the power of the Spirit by faith, how can it teach these things with integrity in words, and how can it teach these things at all by exhibition? And if the church... does not care enough to function in this way as a corporate body in its internal relations, as brothers and sisters in Christ; and then in its external human relationships to those outside the group, how can we expect individual Christians to take these things seriously in their personal lives – in the husband-wife, parent-child, employer-employee, and other relationships?" "True Spirituality," Francis A. Schaeffer, pages 170-1.

"Therefore whoever confesses Me before men, him will I also confess before My Father who is in heaven," But whoever denies Me before men, him I will also deny before My Father who is in heaven," Matthew 10:32-33. How wonderful will it be for you and I to hear, as His disciples, "Well done, good, and faithful servant!"

Chapter 9

What Does It Mean to Believe?

Believing has to do with trust! Do you trust the revealed Word of God? Do you believe in the sufficiency of Scripture?

The Apostle Paul wrote, "All Scripture is given by inspiration of God, and is profitable for doctrine, for reproof, for correction, for instruction in righteousness, that the man of God may be complete, thoroughly equipped for every good work," 2nd Timothy 3:16-17.

Some Pastors, of course, have committed to implement a disciple-making ministry. Many of these same Pastors have, on occasion, observed some of their members engaged for a short time as disciples [trainees] only to amazingly discover for themselves that they were indeed not Christians!

They had neither confessed with their mouth their sins to God, nor had they pleaded for mercy from God or expressed faith in Jesus. "For with the heart one believes unto righteousness, and with the mouth confession is made unto salvation… For whoever calls on the name of the Lord shall be saved," Romans 10:10 & 13.

The lives of many new disciples and disciple makers, not unlike my own, are being transformed. Disciples often times learn what it means to experience great joy as they walk prayerfully. They begin to understand there is a great purpose for regular communion with God and for holiness. There is great joy to be found in obedience to Him.

Chasing the Wind

What does the Bible have to say about those in Church leadership who hold fast to social, political, and or influential contacts while ignoring or overlooking the spiritual gifts given to the ordinary Christian man or woman in their congregation?

Could it be that chasing after the social, political, and influential is attempting to grasp the wind? "Trust in the Lord with all your heart, and lean not on your own understanding; in all your ways acknowledge Him, and He shall direct your paths," Proverbs 3:5.

There seems to be an inherent tendency, especially in many larger Churches, where people in leadership choose others who they think are qualified to be leaders based on social, political, or economic standing in the community. Certainly, God can use anyone He chooses from the greatest to the least. God is no respecter of persons, though in practice, Church polity would and often does differ on that point. Some Church leaders generally favor the nobility, the affluent, and the credentialed in our society for positions of leadership.

Opposition Within the Visible Church

It can be observed in many Churches, the leadership may otherwise not notice the ordinary man or woman who is gifted or called by God. Many Church leaders, not infrequently, choose to ignore those outside their circle of affluence and or influence.

The ordinary person who may want to participate in a particular ministry can be denied that opportunity because it was determined to be a ministry in which the leadership holds no interest. Therefore, that particular ministry does not take wing due to a lack of support by Church leadership.

A good example of this is found in the biography of C. T. Studd. After he had been in Asia for years, he would now respond to the missionary call to Africa. "The doctor's report was absolutely against him. The Committee refused to let me go... They declined to help me to go, withdrawing the funds necessary for such a purpose. Penniless, turned down by the doctor, dropped by the [Church] Committee, yet told by God to go, what was he to do? The only honest thing. Once more he staked all on obedience to God," "C. T. Studd, Cricketer & Pioneer," Norman Grubb, page 120.

There are many ordinary Church members who desire to participate in a discipleship ministry, to be witnesses, and to have a part in the establishment of a gospel ministry. But the leadership intentionally blocks them because, not uncommonly, the leadership itself is not committed to active, sacrificial gospel service in obedience to the Great Commission, at least not in their own hometown.

Yes, there are those in leadership, including Pastors, who will fight against you and your attempts to establish a disciple-making ministry. They are also convinced it is not in the best interest of the Church and they are doing God a favor by opposing any attempt by you to start that ministry.

Further, they may see you as a threat, and in retaliation they may even remove you from your position as Sunday school teacher, or class shepherd. They may also take away your committee responsibilities as an officer and leave you unassigned to any committee as punishment. This may sound secular-political, but it is a reality within Church government where the Great Commission has its opponents!

Sometimes the leadership is more committed to the inward aspects or concerns of an agenda and much less committed to the outward call to "Go therefore and make disciples of all nations…," Matthew 28:19, especially in their local community. Both inwardly and outwardly there is, of course, a need for a balanced ministry. Most of the contemporary Church is noticeably without balance and unashamedly defaulting on disciple making.

Alive to Christ

Today, it is common to be systematically isolated by Church leadership, and possibly ridiculed for your desire and enthusiasm for disciple making. A very dear friend of mine lost his Church, as he explained, because of those in leadership who were predisposed to humanistic ideals. It seemed the Bible was little more than a book of suggestions to those in leadership. My friend was the Senior Pastor before his Church leadership fired him.

His dedication to preaching, teaching, biblical authority, and sufficiency of Scripture was an affront to the leadership, especially to many women in the Church. He explained to me that it seemed the women in his former Church were running it, and those Elders on the session were little more than puppets who were controlled by these women. The social concerns of that Church, he explained, appeared to trump things spiritual.

By grace, God used this man as he continued to make himself available, though many Churches rejected him. Several years passed by and this widower, with four children, was invited to participate in the Evangelism Explosion ["EE"] disciple-making ministry in Asia. Note: D. James Kennedy of the Coral Ridge Presbyterian Church, P.C.A., Fort Lauderdale, Florida founded the EE ministry.

This gentle, loving, and quiet man believed in the promises of God. He confided to me that he trusted God alone for the results. He made it a point to ask only God, and no one else, to make physical provision for him and his family. God honored his request. His faith and prayer petitions, in practice, seemed reminiscent of what I had read concerning George Muller of Great Britain who lived about a century ago.

This remarkable man was outwardly quiet, humble, and a loyal friend. He seemed grateful for everything. God enabled him to train literally thousands of Pastors and Elders in 15 Asian countries. His full-time ministry was to train those who dedicated themselves to making disciples of others.

His excitement grew exponentially. After approximately 10 years in the disciple-making ministry, the gospel was reaching an estimated 43,000 people per day! Whatever the numbers, it is reasonable to expect that all who heard the gospel message did not repent and believe it. However, there were multitudes that did make that decision and commitment. Multitudes of new believers became disciples and subsequently disciple makers themselves. To God be the glory!

The joy of my friend grew to amazing proportions. Muslims targeted him for assassination. The Christian Church in Asia held his name in high regard. They saw his personal commitment to Christ and the Great Commission, which was propelled by the Spirit of God, actively moving across Asia.

His former Church had no clue that God would take this ordinary, quiet person, one who trusted the Word of God, and make of him a good and faithful servant. My friend is now with the Lord. His ministry continues to thrive, not because of him. It thrives because of whom he believed. He believed in the living God who does all things well! He understood that, as a steward, when one holds up the gospel of our Lord, God draws all men to Himself. Would that Pastors and Church leadership would understand and respond accordingly. It is Jehovah God who builds His Church! Those who are called to be a disciple, and then a disciple maker, taste of the good things of the Lord that nothing else can satisfy or match.

Revival in the Heart

While continuing on life's journey, self-examination for the disciple becomes routine. Confession, forgiveness received, and deep gratitude for our Lord's mercy generally precedes spiritual growth.

Disciples find themselves looking around to see where God is at work. They join Him in that work. That is what Jesus did. He came to do the work of His Father. Often difficulty confronts the disciple, even in his own Church, especially when the leadership blocks his effort to establish or assist in a disciple-making ministry.

The opportunity to win souls will still come. It comes often and most of the time in casual circumstances. Soul winning is always glorious and pleasing to God. Joy inexpressible refreshes the soul of the messenger to see the visible evidence of the Holy Spirit at work in the world of the lost.

The Holy Spirit works in the disciple and in the disciple maker as they testify of Jesus, and as they proclaim the good news of the gospel. It is an awesome and humbling privilege! Jesus explained, "I say to you that likewise there will be more joy in heaven over one sinner who repents than over ninety-nine just persons who need no repentance," Luke 15:7.

Dear Reader, within the United States and in this present age, there is a severe drought of things spiritual. As in the days of Noah, men are doing what is right in their own eyes. Men accuse others of what they themselves are guilty of and they excuse themselves of sin and guilt without hesitation. Their deepest presuppositions seem to be limited to what is expedient for them. Conversion of souls to our Lord in the United States today seems to be rare.

Many in government and in Church leadership appear to seek what is convenient to some philosophical agenda and they ignore what the Scripture commands. Repentance toward God and faith in His Son Jesus is the great need of our country. The contemporary Church itself oftentimes seems to waffle between two or more opinions under confused and sometimes chaotic leadership. Jonathan Edwards in his examination of the Church in his day wrote, "That God would pour out his Spirit upon us, and revive His work in the midst of the years," "Jonathan Edwards on Revival, page 77. Amen.

Chapter 10

Biblical Leadership
or Status Quo?

The Church has within itself a remnant, which God has preserved for Himself. "Even so then, at this present time there is a remnant according to the election of grace," Romans 11:5.

A revival within the Church can become reality when the Church pleads "O Lord, revive Thy work in the midst of the years – Wilt thou revive us again, that Thy people may rejoice in Thee?" "The Welsh Revival," Thomas Phillips, page 3. The Israel of God and that remnant in the Church today, needs hold fast to the promise, "Then you will call upon Me and go and pray to Me, and I will listen to you. And you will seek Me and find Me, when you search for Me with all your heart. I will be found by you, says the Lord, I will bring you back from your captivity..." Jeremiah 29:12-14

God changes not. His mercy endures forever. Most of the Church in the United States does not appear to be searching for God with their whole heart. It, therefore, must repent of its sinful ways and return to Jesus.

Prayer, and Revival

The Church must begin again to catechize children and whole families. It must train, send, and support missionaries. Its anchor must be the study of Holy Scripture to show itself approved and not to be ashamed. It must trust in God who began a good work in His Church, and it is only God who is able to complete it.

The Church must take up its cross, go into its own Jerusalem, and engage its neighbors with love. By holding up the gospel of Jesus, men will be drawn to the Lord by the Spirit. The local Church must be sowing the gospel in their own hometown, winsomely engaging its neighbors, and walking in the Spirit.

"Prayer now becomes something more than merely an abstract religious, devotional act. It is a place where the Church is the Church and where Christ is in the midst in a special, definite, and real way. Organization is not wrong; let us say this with force, organization is clearly commanded in the Word of God, and it is needed in a fallen world. But it becomes wrong if it stands in the way of the conscious relationship of the Church to Christ," "True Spirituality," Francis Schaeffer, page 174. The exhortation from Jesus to Peter was, "Feed My sheep!" God can use an unschooled fisherman to accomplish His purpose. "Jesus said to him [Peter] feed my sheep," John 21:17. God can make the ordinary, the quiet, and the humble Church member, who makes himself available to God, useable. Church leadership must prayerfully, thoughtfully, and intentionally equip and deploy the laity.

"Had it pleased the Sovereign of His Church to choose the learned, the intellectual, the eloquent, to take the lead in [a] revival, the temptation would be still greater to say, 'This is the work of man. Those who are best acquainted with the work, especially as it bears upon the personal character of multitudes are most ready to acknowledge – 'A greater Man is here!' " "The Welsh Revival," Thomas Phillips, page 132.

Prayer meetings have been the principal means whereby a Church is awakened. I am, not unlike others, persuaded that the means blessed of God to create and carry on revival is prayer. Someone observed during the great revival in Wales that amazingly, those who are not known for eloquence become exceedingly so before the throne of grace.

A new attitude toward Sunday and keeping it holy makes a Church congregation a great example within its community. Sunday should not be just another day in the week. It is a day made for man, set aside for worship of the living God who by grace redeems us.

Leadership in Name Only

Will we have real leadership in the Church again? Though there are some leaders of good report, there are still many more who reside in the status quo. The club-like atmosphere in some Churches is reminiscent of those who run the typical American corporation.

Leadership within the Church is in many instances reflective of modern corporate America. The Church body, rather than choosing men who demonstrate godliness in their family and professional lives, often chooses those who have substantial visibility in corporate America, or tend to be affluent, to lead in the Church.

Those in leadership within the Church have oversight and, therefore, review candidates nominated for office. Many Pastors and leaders, not surprisingly, tend to choose candidates based on something other than biblical prescription found in Titus and 1st Timothy.

Sadly, there are numerous officers elected by the Church who will purposely avoid teaching Bible or Catechism. Many of these leaders will not become involved in discipleship personally. Some Church leaders will actually block those who seek to implement a discipleship ministry. These Church leaders are not up to it personally, and will not tolerate it in others for reasons of their own making. However, the Church leader, who first becomes a disciple, accepts responsibility, and undertakes personal accountability for those things the Lord has given to him, is in the path of obedience. Discipleship requires study, personal time devoted to learning Scripture, and a willingness to go into the community, in one venue or another, and there to become a witness and to proclaim the gospel of Jesus.

From Disciple to Disciple Maker

Ultimately, the disciple becomes more and more of a role model for others. Mentoring becomes a part of his or her periodic routine. Bible teaching, exhorting, encouraging, prayer, and soul winning increasingly become a joyous part of his or her life. A disciple's heart is made glad in the Lord!

The Church leader and disciple now becomes the disciple maker. He understands he has become a servant of all, not just to his family, to his Church, but to his neighbor and even the stranger. His delight is in making himself available to the Lord, knowing that He can make him useable. He becomes a Jew to the Jew and a Greek to the Greek, not wanting to be an offense to any man. He knows that he need not fear the faces of men because the Lord God of all flesh prepares the hearts of those who will respond to the gospel.

Shocking, but true, the disciple maker becomes much more aware of the opposition to the gospel. Much of the opposition can be found in the ranks of the Church leadership! However, where sin abounds, grace abounds much more! The disciple-maker is called to contend for the faith.

People may or may not be looking for the truth. But many people are looking for hope and light.
The slumbering evangelical leadership, in numerous local Churches, has not discipled its membership. They are absent without leave, AWOL!

Therefore, the Mormons, the Jehovah's Witness, and Muslim groups are quick to grasp the opportunity. They knock on doors all over America and ask permission to witness. Consequently, the resident finds himself listening to something other than the biblical gospel of Jesus.

The disciple maker understands the explanation from Scripture, "And how shall they preach unless they are sent?...," Romans 10:15. "And when He brings out His own sheep, He goes before them; and the sheep follow Him, for they know His voice," John 10:4.

Does the leadership in your Church train its membership in discipleship and disciple making? Are those in leadership positions demonstrating obedience to the Great Commission? Does your leadership know and follow the voice of the Master into their Jerusalem?

Chapter 11

Necessity for Accountability in Wartime

Suitable to the occasion for Church preaching are exhortations, warnings, and direction. Many Pastors do not preach with a sense of urgency! Often times Pastors preach the same line, as if mowing the lawn once a week. It is just something they do each week as a matter of routine. Soul saving is far removed from the agenda of some Pastors as evidenced by their monologue. Consequently, there is an absence of power in the preaching of those Pastors! Hate of sin and love for sinners is less than apparent.

Many Pastors in the pulpit sometimes make assumptions. Some may assume that the audience has heard and understood the gospel from past sermons. Therefore, it is no longer necessary to remind the congregation of what is in store for those who have not repented of sin. The necessity for the sinner to approach God by faith and earnestly seek forgiveness of sin by the blood of Jesus may not even be mentioned in the sermon, let alone be emphasized!

Pastors, "The work of God must needs be done! Souls must not perish, while you mind your worldly business or worldly pleasure, and take your ease, or quarrel with your brethren! Nor must we be silent while men are hastened by you to perdition, and the Church brought into greater danger and confusion, for fear of seeming too uncivil and unmannerly with you, or displeasing your impatient souls! If you will enter into the office of ministry, which is for the necessary preservation of us all, so that by letting you alone in your sin, we must give up the Church to loss and hazard, blame us not if we talk to you more freely than you would have us do," "The Reformed Pastor," Richard Baxter, page 40.

Community Organizer or Pastor?

Some Pastors are frequently tempted to say something from the pulpit about themselves or their families. Many are the Pastors who apparently speak with amusement in mind. Isn't the Pastor now the center of attention rather than the gospel message? Some Pastors, apparently, do not perceive that there may be a one-time visitor from out of town or an infrequent local visitor who never understood his or her depraved situation before the Holy God of Israel. Consequently, the gospel, if presented at all, is less than clear and the sermon is devoid of urgency! Why does the typical Pastor not take aim at the conscience each week? Would that be out of order? It would be in order, in my opinion, for Churches who profess to be evangelical! "How beautiful upon the mountains are the feet of him who brings good news, who proclaims peace, who brings glad tidings of good things, who proclaims salvation, who says to Zion, 'Your God reigns!' " Isaiah 52:7.

Some Pastors fear the Church leadership might reprimand them if they told the congregation their sins to their faces! Jesus very often spoke of hell and the eternal torment for those who choose not to repent and believe on Him. It is, therefore, very important to confront sin.

Pastors have an influence on family leadership. Could it be that some parents model the Pastor on occasion by not confronting their own children concerning sin?

Accountability at the Top

Additionally, a system of leadership in the local Church that lacks a discipleship ministry and fails to perpetuate an active, intentional disciple-making ministry is negligent of the Great Commission. That too, in my view, is sin! Church leadership is responsible, not only for establishing a discipleship ministry, but to unequivocally require all those who are nominated for the office of Elder to understand clearly they will be required to participate in that ministry. They are required to be 'apt to teach' and should be expected to teach the members in Bible, catechism instruction, and discipleship ministry.

I've known many Elders who do not engage in teaching Bible. Many do not routinely share their testimony or the gospel with others outside the Church. Their office has become something other than what it was intended. The reality for disciple making is that we are on wartime footing! Time is of the essence. "Whereas you do not know what will happen tomorrow. For what is your life? It is even a vapor that appears for a little time and then vanishes away," James 4:14.

The Church leader must himself first become a disciple. He is expected to understand and solemnly commit to practice his Christian testimony. He must be able to thoughtfully articulate the gospel of our Lord in a winsome manner as he engages others.

Men nominated for Church leadership positions ought to hear a clear explanation of what is expected of them in the regular performance of their responsibilities, first as a disciple and then as a disciple maker, if they are elected to serve. The disciple maker is responsible for the teaching and training of disciples who in turn should have an eye toward training the next generation of disciple makers.

Don't miss this point! Pastors, Bishops, Elders and Deacons, are not going to implement, perpetuate, and persevere in disciple making without the Senior Pastor and Senior leadership being involved in this ministry. Senior Pastors cannot delegate away a primary responsibility that is theirs! Implementation and accountability for this ministry runs to the top without exception. Jesus did not avoid His responsibility and the Senior Pastor must not! "And being found in appearance as a man, He humbled Himself and became obedient to the point of death, even the death of the cross," Philippians 2:8. If your Senior Pastor does not have the stomach or commitment for active, intentional disciple making, which includes evangelism outside of the church building, then I suggest you prayerfully reconsider whom you have in that position! Why reconsider? Because the biblical model for disciple making is Jesus.

Prayer Precedes Activity

Jesus taught His disciples how to pray and when to pray. He was the example. He was here to do the work of His Father. Other ideas for ministry were secondary! He took His disciples everywhere. He demonstrated what to do and how to do it. Prayer and expectation of what the Father would accomplish through Him always preceded activity. He did not restrict or limit His teaching to the synagogue, as most contemporary Pastors seem to do.

Building on the Rock-of-Ages

The Holy Spirit, which proceeds from the Father and the Son, is given to us in the Church. We are to be about the work given to us by the Spirit. What is that work?

Go into the entire world and make disciples! It is not just about sending out missionaries to other countries, though that is part of it. It is not just about teaching a class on evangelism, though that too is very important.

The Church leadership that sets the standard for disciple making as a priority and requires accountability of itself and its members is almost ready for battle. The Lord promised never to leave you and is ready to work in and through the person who makes himself available to Him, as demonstrated in the life of David. The battle, however, is the Lord's! "Then all this assembly shall know that the Lord does not save with sword and spear; for the battle is the Lord's, and He will give you into our hands," 1st Samuel 17:47.

He will go with you and before you to make your way straight. Success is measured in the degree to which we are obedient to the Lord. We are called to be obedient to Him and not to a program or any other person or thing. Discipleship anticipates you reaching your own Jerusalem. Your Jerusalem is your neighborhood, your family, and your local circle of influence. Do not delude yourself by thinking that, if I send out missionaries, then my duty is done!

An example of that misguided mindset is the failure observed in the European Church model. The European Church leaders failed to become disciples first and consequently failed to become disciple makers. Church discipline was generally ignored and European congregations, in general, did not require accountability of their Church leadership for disciples making.

Europeans did not perpetuate their witness and subsequently they failed to preach the gospel; as evidenced by what the Church has lost in Europe. The consequence of disobedience to the Great Commission in Europe resulted in the disappearance of

God-fearing Churches, whole congregations, and eventually God-fearing governments.

"For I am not ashamed of the gospel of Christ, for it is the power of God to salvation for every one who believes, for the Jew first and also for the Greek," Romans 1:16. Where Jesus Christ is lifted up, the Holy Spirit draws whom He will. Souls will be saved. The local Church in America must establish its foundation on none other than Jesus of Nazareth.

God is thereby glorified and the Church typically grows in depth and in numbers when biblical discipleship is implemented. "Righteousness exalts a nation, but sin is a reproach to any people," Proverbs 14:34.

Can there be any doubt that the lack of a biblical-based, disciple-making ministry in the Church in America has resulted in us becoming more like European progressives? The large cathedrals of Europe have become more monument-like, even museums of yester-year.

Bread of Life

Most of the European Churches have become, through succeeding generations, houses that have lost their first love, and are no longer houses of prayer and worship of God Almighty. "If we had more life and earnestness in the pulpit, then there would be far more life and holiness in the congregation," "The Welsh Revival," Thomas Phillips, page 38.

"And to the angel of the church of the Laodiceans write... I know your works, that you are neither cold nor hot... So then, because you are lukewarm, and neither cold nor hot, I will vomit you out of My Mouth. Because you say, 'I am rich, have become wealthy, and need of nothing' – and do not know that you are wretched, miserable, poor, blind, and naked...
As many as I love, I rebuke and chasten. Therefore be zealous and repent. Behold, I stand at the door and knock. If any man hears My voice and opens the door, I will come in to him and dine with him, and he with Me." To him who overcomes I will grant to sit with Me on My throne... He who has an ear, let him hear what the Spirit says to the churches," Revelation 3:14-17, 19-22.

Listen to these words from Proverbs 30:4. "Who has ascended into heaven, or descended? Who hath gathered the wind in His fists? Who has bound the waters in a garment? Who has established all the ends of the earth? What is His name, and what is His Son's name, if you know?" It is Jehovah God! It is Jesus the Christ! It is the Savior of sinners who is not known by most United States citizens!

Very few lost people hear the gospel in the market place or in the public schools of the United States, or in most towns today. Most Pastors and Church leaders in America, as we pointed out, are not deploying disciples or disciple makers into their hometown! When did someone last approach you in your community, outside of your church, who asked permission to share his or her testimony and or the gospel with you?

Think about it! How many folks have you observed in your community who are fulfilling the Great Commission outside of your church? How will they, your neighbors, friends, and associates call upon Him of whom they have not heard? And how will they hear without the gospel?

Dear Church leader, the Bread of Life needs to be taken out of the breadbox that you keep inside your Church walls. If not now, when? If not through your obedience, then by and through whom will it be given?

Be the exceptional Pastor, Elder, or Deacon and trust God to give you a heart for the lost in your Jerusalem. "Then He [Jesus] said to them, "The harvest truly is great, but the laborers are few; therefore pray the Lord of the harvest to send out laborers into His harvest," Luke10:2.

Chapter 12

Counting the Cost;
Making the Commitment

The high school and university student in the United
States of America is typically encouraged to keep an
open mind regarding every issue of life. It sounds like
good advice. However, the critical thinking person
further qualifies that advice and adds that an open mind
should never be an empty mind for important reasons.

I once read the issues of life need sound
presuppositions with which to test accurate solutions,
rightness and wrongness, justice and injustice. It made
sense to me. Someone pointed out, if we want to test a
scientific question in the lab, then we can test one
chemical with another. If we have a math problem,
then we may apply certain theorems. If we have a
question pertaining to logic, then we may begin with a
specific hypothesis. If we have a legal question, then
we ought to consult a lawyer or search for a precedent.

But how do we test moral questions or validate religion? What does it mean to have faith? Are there absolute laws and moral laws that impose a consequence? These kinds of questions demanded the attention of our forefathers because the answers would be foundational to our form of government, our system of jurisprudence, its economy, and ultimately individual freedoms.

Some individuals gratuitously assert that faith is a means for encouragement and that all religions are the same. However, upon close examination, the Jewish and Christian faiths are not merely religions. There are distinct differences between the 'people of the book' and other world religions.

Christianity & Jewish Faiths Vs. World Religions

Alistair Begg defines some religious differences, "The Jews believe the Messiah is yet to come. We [Christians] believe He has already come. He is Jesus. We cannot both be right. Islam believes that Allah is god and he has no son. We [Christians] believe Allah is Satan and Jesus is God the Son. We cannot both be right. Buddhists believe in many reincarnations. We believe only Jesus is the incarnate God. We cannot both be right. Hindus believe there are many ways to God. We believe Jesus is the only Way. We cannot both be right."

The Jewish and Christian faiths are reflective of personal relationships with God. The Jews continue to look for the Messiah. This was prophesied in the TENAK or Old Testament, which explained the Jews would not recognize Him at His first appearing but at His Second Coming.

The Christian, on the other hand, believes that Jesus is the Messiah who is coming back and bringing judgment to the nations with Him. The prophecy from the TENAK, written centuries beforehand, that believing Gentiles would be engrafted into the body of Israel would be and is being fulfilled.

Christianity has to do with eternal relationships that begin with God, by grace, through faith in Jesus Christ and His 'finished work' of redemption on the cross. World religions, by contrast, are all in some form or fashion a means for man to earn a place in heaven or some approval from God. The God of the Bible, as testified to in numerous historical accounts, in specific times and places, has revealed Himself and His plan for redemption.

Christianity is faith in what God has revealed about himself in Jesus Christ and about us. "Now faith is the substance of things hoped for, the evidence of things not seen," Hebrews 11:1. Hope is counted as certain expectation. Belief means to put trust in some person or thing.

As contrasted with worldly religions, Christianity is about God reaching down to a lost world. It is not about man's epic adventure to seek after God. It is about literally hundreds of documented prophecies written over many centuries that preceded events;

specific details that actually came to pass that we know today as history. Probability science is overwhelmed by the detailed accuracy of biblical prophecy. The careful student of the Bible is in awe of the majestic authority and God–given assurances revealed by the Holy Spirit. There are not any worldly religions that have prophecy to substantiate or authenticate them. At best, they have man – made traditions!

When students question, "What is truth?" the presupposition evident in the question is that the answer must be in some thing. However, in reality the 'truth' is a person. Jesus said to him, "I am the way, the truth, and the life. No one comes to the Father except through Me," John 14:6.

The apostle John records, "In the beginning was the Word, and the Word was with God, and the Word was God … and we beheld His glory, the glory as of the only begotten of the Father, full of grace and truth," John 1:1, 14.

Choose Whom You Will Serve

All of this is to say that each person has his or her own presuppositions with which to render a decision. We are cognitive beings who think. We are volitional beings who make choices. We are spiritual beings with a mind, a will and emotions. My own presuppositions start with the 'first cause' or God. The 'plumb line' of purity is Jesus Christ. "For I am not ashamed of the gospel of Christ, for it is the power of God to salvation for everyone who believes, for the Jew first and also for the Greek," Romans 1:16.

It is my observation that one of the most difficult responsibilities for men and women to come to terms with, in the body life of the Church, is that of discipleship. Jesus is the model given to us in the New Testament. He took His disciples everywhere to demonstrate what it meant to be a disciple. He taught His disciples for three years until it became a way-of-life ministry for them.

Discipleship requires a daily surrendering to our Lord. "He must increase, but I must decrease," John 3:30. "Nor is there salvation in any other, for there is no other name under heaven given among men by which we must be saved," Acts 4:12. What follows next is the Great Commission. Jesus cautioned his disciples not to worry about what they would say. "But when they deliver you up, do not worry about how or what you should speak. For it will be given to you in that hour what you should speak; for it is not you who speak, but the Spirit of your Father who speaks in you," Matthew 10:19-20.

Again, the Spirit explains concerning God's word, "So shall My word be that goes forth from My mouth; it shall not return unto me void, but it shall accomplish what I please, and it shall prosper in the thing for which I sent it," Isaiah 55:11.

Going on to Maturity

A word to fellow Pastors, Elders and Deacons - Jesus is the standard for you and for me. We have all fallen short. But take heart! The work that He has begun in you and me, He is able to complete! You and I are called to serve God rather than man. Joshua exhorted Israel, "…Choose for your selves this day whom you will serve… But as for me and my house, we will serve the Lord," Joshua 24:15.

Let us join Him in His work that He may be glorified and that our joy may be full in Him. If you are not already a disciple maker, then become one today and serve God in a larger capacity, as you are led by the Holy Spirit to do so.

Trust in Him to accomplish in your ministry all He has purposed for you before the foundation of the world. He is able to show you great and mighty things that you haven't even imagined! "Behold, I am the Lord, the God of all flesh. Is there anything too hard for me?" Jeremiah 32:27.

"God is only known in the soul as we yield ourselves to Him, submit to His authority, and regulate all the details of our lives by His holy precepts and commandments." "The Attributes of God," Arthur W. Pink, page 7.

Warren Wiersbe explains with reference to Hebrews 6:1, "The ABC's of the Christian life are important, but they must be a launching pad and not a parking lot, for the challenge is, 'Let us go on to Maturity.' If we get sluggish and dull toward the Word, we may fall by the wayside and stop being fruitful. As long as disobedient believers are bringing shame to Christ, it is impossible to bring them to repentance, and God must deal with them," "With the Word," page 817.

"Let us know, let us pursue the knowledge of the Lord… (in the path of obedience)," Hosea 6:3. "If any one wills to do His will, he shall know… " John 7:17. "The people who know their God shall be strong…" Daniel 11:32.

Anthony Hoekema exhorts us forward in our responsibility toward our nation, "We [as Christians] must be active in the political arena, through the efforts of Christian legislators, judges and magistrates; the ballot box, petitions, and referendums; through bringing pressure to bear on elected officials," "Created in God's Image," page 201.

Disciple Making Opportunities

Not unlike many others, I served in the U.S. Navy four years and I am grateful for all the benefits and individual freedoms that our nation secures for us by way of a Constitutional Republic. But more over, "Blessed is the nation whose God is the Lord, The people He has chosen as His own inheritance," Psalm 33:12.

Lest I forget, the Youth Minister has an exciting opportunity within the Church. While some Churches are blessed with a Senior Pastor who is committed to disciple making and other Churches are not, nevertheless, the Youth Minister has a unique and privileged opportunity.

The Children's "First Catechism" with its 145 questions and answers are foundational to what it is that Christian's believe. The knowledge in this book serves as an explanation of doctrinal information that becomes a foundation with which the youth can anchor their presuppositions for a Christian world-life view.

It will not take the place of Scripture, nor should it. But it provides a means of learning for young minds of what Scripture explains. The structure and content are drawn from the "Catechism for Young Children," originally published in 1840 by Joseph P. Engels. In short, it simplifies the "Westminster Shorter Catechism."

The Youth Minister may ask where is a good place to start with children in learning the Scripture and at what age? My personal experience is that small children can learn all 145 answers to the Children's "First Catechism" while in kindergarten. But it must be fortified or reviewed from year–to–year, as they grow older.

The reality of children's or Youth Ministry is that we have children coming and going from one church to another because their parents have moved. Nevertheless, the point is to teach essential doctrine while you have them.

The Children's "First Catechism" is also a means for drawing in the participation and support by the parents. Hold your expectations above the ankle, above the knee, above the waist and above the eyebrow!

Middle school students are in formative years and respond to effective leadership. Again, hold your expectations high. Pray for them first! Catechize them next! Over the span of three or four years, a student can experience many blessings that accompany obedience to our Lord. They can and should study, but they should also experience a level of 'reality' that no worldly religion can imitate. Visit each young person and their family, by appointment, at least once a year. Draw in the parents through in-home visitation and prayer. Explain the importance and the essentials of learning the catechism to parents. Your ministry is a demonstration of the love that Jesus had for children.

Organize students into learning groups. Again: Pray for them first! Catechize them second! Third, when a student completes all of their catechism in one sitting, then award them publically with a Bible in front of the congregation.

Next, help the middle school and high school student to develop his or her own two-minute personal testimony. Do not assume any of your students are regenerate or born again. This step helps the student to do self-examination. It also challenges their understanding. It allows them to ask questions and assimilate information that they may have not explored before. Developing a testimony gives the high school and middle school student a chance to be grounded and to declare what they believe, mainly what it means to be a Christian. They may want to articulate in their testimony what it was like before they became a Christian and what life is like now after becoming a Christian.

Now you have before you a potential young disciple candidate who has begun growing into maturity, progressing from milk to meat, and one who is able to glorify our Father in heaven. Discipleship may soon become a way-of-life for that young person.

Not surprisingly, would you believe many middle school and high school children who have progressed to this step have a keener understanding of doctrinal truths than many adults in the congregation? Now is the time for them to learn to articulate the Roman Road or the Four Spiritual Laws to enable them to be an effective witness.

Practice, practice, and more practice are not just a recipe for the young musician to someday arrive at Carnegie Hall. Practice helps the young Christian to articulate the gospel. Practice helps him or her to question his own testimony and to advance his or her understanding. Practice is a means to encourage him or her in making the commitment to become a disciple of the Lord.

Chapter 13

Ministry Structure and Preparation for Spiritual Battle

"I beseech you therefore, brethren, by the mercies of God..." Romans 12:1. The Apostle to the Gentiles, with gentle but firm and earnest persuasion admonished and exhorted the Church to not be conformed to this world.

My motivation for admonishing, exhorting, and encouraging leadership in the Church toward the calling to make disciples goes back to who gave the command. That motivation has also been stimulated by an observable falling away from Scriptural precepts as evidenced throughout the Church in the United States. Likewise, the Church has had a less than stellar example to display for American society and government.

Many Churches have a liberal prism through which leaders view Scripture. The Bible is not authoritative in the view of many. The political correctness of the culture often bleeds over into the Church and subverts biblical precepts. Sin is not something Church members want to talk about or acknowledge. The Church may appear to be a mile wide in membership, but most of it is only an inch deep in biblical understanding.

The wolves within the Church, who are not submissive as disciples themselves, detract from the urgency of the command. They were not disciples and are therefore not qualified disciple makers. These so-called leaders prevent others from maturing in the faith. A secularized leadership presence in the Church is not committed to making disciples. They are determined and will knowingly attempt to stifle others who raise the banner of obedience to the Lord with respect to His Great Commission for every believer.

The remnant within the Church is still called to obedience today. Disciple making is always found in the path of obedience. Obedience out of gratitude to our loving Savior comes from knowing we were bought with a price, the richest treasure that heaven had to offer. "There are occasions sovereignly chosen by God, when this same Holy Spirit allows greater degrees of His power upon the preached Word and, through that Word, upon believers. And this is revival," "The Beddgelert Revival," Eryl Davies, page 135.

Precepts to build upon:

> Intentional, individualized mentoring of those who are able to teach others

<u>Awareness</u>, the weapons of our warfare are spiritual, not carnal

Learn <u>how to pray</u> from Scripture; Spirit led petitions

<u>Intentional discipleship</u>, our planned and executed response to the great commission

<u>Availability</u> for training of men and women for two semesters at a minimum

<u>Accountability,</u> the way to build up others, as iron sharpens iron

<u>Learning</u> Bible precepts for winsomely <u>engaging others without fear</u>

<u>Bible Study</u>, to show us approved... workmen who need not be ashamed

<u>Apologetics</u>, "What does it means to Believe"

<u>Individual testimony</u> development; a two-minute explanation to others

<u>Modeling evangelism</u>, 'a ready witness' demonstrates "how to" to disciple the intern

<u>Prayer in a frequent, disciplined manner</u>; where two or more are gathered together...

<u>Life-style discipleship</u> engages the family, our associates, our neighbors, visitors, and strangers, all within our Jerusalem

Church officers <u>visit every church member</u> in their home at least once a year

<u>Visit every first – time 'visitor'</u> to the church within one week (local resident)

Determine who or what are <u>prospective church members</u> trusting in for salvation

Help others <u>identify spiritual gifts</u> within the body of the church

These job descriptions are a guide for a Church that has an earnest commitment for the Disciple-making ministry and the involvement of 60 or more people in its ministry.

Director of Discipleship:

- Reports directly to the Session Elders or Board of Deacons.

- Manages the disciple-making ministry.

- Recruit two prayer partners with whom he prays each week.

- Develops and manages the administrative processes for the ministry.

- Selects key lay-team personnel and managers for team positions.

- Assigns ministry implementation plans.

- Responsible for disciple-maker certification.

- Participates on in-home visitation.

Associate Pastor / Discipleship:

- Works with and supports the Director of Discipleship.

- Responsible for the nomination of the Liaison Elder and Liaison Deacon.

- Recruits two prayer partners with whom he prays each week.

- Models disciple making and participates in ministry in-home visitation.

- Encourages participation by the congregation into the discipleship ministry.

- Acts as Liaison between the home Church and sister Churches in discipleship.

Manager / Prayer Ministry:

- Recruits two prayer partners with whom he prays each week.

- Works with and reports directly to the Director of Discipleship.

- Responsible for organization of the prayer ministry.

- Tracks regular participation by disciples and disciple makers in prayer ministry.

- Requires two prayer partners for each Disciple and Disciple maker.

- Interviews and qualifies Disciples for the two-semester commitments.

- Coordinates prayer partner attendance for one evening church prayer service.

- Qualifies prayer partners into prospect trainees for next semester.

- Participates as a Disciple-maker for in-home visitation.

- Co-ordinates with Manager–Hospitality on end-of-semester, testimonial dinner.

Teacher of Discipleship:

- Works with and reports directly to the Director of Discipleship.

- Recruits two prayer partners with whom he prays each week.

- Teaches biblical precepts of discipleship, testimony development, and gospel.

- Teaches essentials for being certified competent at the end of the semester.

- Participates on in-home visitation.

Co-Teacher of Discipleship:

- Reports directly to the Director of Discipleship.

- Recruits two prayer partners with whom he or she prays each week.

- Teaches biblical precepts of discipleship as assigned by Lead-Teacher.

- Participates on in-home visitation.

Supervisor of Visitation Assignments & Contact Reporting:

- Reports directly to the Director of Discipleship.

- Recruits two prayer partners with whom he or she prays each week.

- Tracks Church membership attendance and local visitor attendance.

- Assigns weekly visitation contacts to each three-person team.

- Maintains close communication with the Diaconate Liaison.

- Ensures visitation assignments are made and reports by teams are completed.

- Submits a weekly report to Director of Discipleship regarding visitation.

Elder Liaison:

- Must certify as a Disciple maker.

- Works with and reports directly to the Director of Discipleship.

- Recruits two prayer partners with whom he prays each week.

- Makes in-home visits to follow up after a profession of faith.

- Functions as a Disciple maker in a relief capacity if any team leader is absent.

Diaconate Liaison:

- Works with and reports directly to the Director of Discipleship.

- Recruits two prayer partners with whom he prays each week.

- Must certify as a Disciple maker.

- Functions as a Disciple maker in a relief capacity if any team leader is absent.

- Serves as a backup in the absence of the Supervisor of Visitation.

- Works on follow up for in-home visitation to a profession of faith.

Music Leader:

- Works with and reports directly to the Director of Discipleship.

- Provides accompaniment for worshipful singing prior to classroom lectures.

- Attends end of semester dinner and is in charge of the worship music.

- Recruits two prayer partners with whom he or she prays each week.

- Serves as a backup in the absence of the Manager of the Prayer Ministry.

Supervisor Hospitality:

- Works with and reports directly to the Director of Discipleship.

- Recruits two prayer partners with whom he or she prays each week.

- Plans the end-of-semester program dinner and co-ordinates special functions.

Co-coordinator of Disciple-Makers Council:

- Appointed by the Director of Discipleship.

- Must have been a certified Disciple maker for at least two semesters.

- Coordinates a monthly fellowship for the Captains of Trainers.

- Coaches Disciple-makers on how to make progress reports.

Captains of Trainers:

- Devoted to tactical development of a group of trainers in discipleship ministry.

- Appointed by and report only to the Director of Discipleship.

- Assigned to exercise practical and helpful oversight on two to five teams.

- Makes weekly contacts with the team leaders only, in person or by telephone.

- Determines when did each Disciple maker pray last with prayer partners?

- Determines when did each Trainee pray last with prayer partners?
- What were the results of the current week's visitation telephone calls, if any?

- Determines what were the results of the current week's visitation contacts.

- Determines how many professions of faith were made.

- Determines how many folks prayed for assurance.

- Describes actual progress of each trainee.

- Determines what follow-up action was made following in-home visits.

- Prays with and for each team-leader every week!

Conclusion

I will not quarrel with those in Church leadership who put off or avoid their responsibility to the command to make disciples. I desire sincerely to persuade as many in Church leadership, as the Lord pleases, to act in obedience to the high calling of discipleship and disciple making.

"And a servant of the Lord must not quarrel but be gentle to all, able to teach, patient, in humility correcting those who are in opposition, if God perhaps will grant them repentance, so that they may know the truth, and that they may come to their senses and escape the snare of the devil, having been taken captive by him to do his will,"
2nd Timothy 2:24-26.

The ordinary and routine events of life are set before the leadership in the Church. We, in leadership, may choose to serve the Lord or become self-absorbed with our own agenda that is the sin of idolatry of one sort or another.

Each opportunity given in our lives is being lived to its fullest when we make ourselves available to Him who makes us useable as a disciple.

More than Evangelism

Discipleship and disciple making is a way-of-life ministry to others. "But be doers of the word, and not hearers only, deceiving yourselves. For if anyone is a hearer of the word and not a doer, he is like a man observing his natural face in a mirror; for he observes himself, goes away, and immediately forgets what kind of man he was," James 1:22-24.

Disciple making involves a great deal of close mentoring. Love is the prime motivator. Again, don't miss this point; evangelism by itself is not disciple making! Disciple making includes evangelism, but disciple making is so much more than evangelism.

Disciple making intentionally brings the candle out from under the Church's bushel that was hidden in the basement. It intentionally sets the gospel and the power of the resurrection of Jesus Christ upon a pedestal for everyone in the local community to see. Disciple making is always intentional, profoundly relational, and individualized to those we are privileged to witness to and to teach.

Disciple making requires regular Bible study, Scripture memory work, personal testimony development, accountability to others over time, frequent prayer ministry involvement, and the confidence that God's word will not return unto Him void.

At the core, disciple making is abiding in Him who is always faithful. It pleases Him [Jesus] to show us great and mighty things that we haven't thought of, or imagined.

"I am the vine, you are the branches. He who abides in Me, and I in him, bears much fruit; for without Me you can do nothing," John 15:5.

The constant in the discipleship ministry is the inspired word of God, the Bible.

Apprehend the Means of Grace

What about discipleship and evangelism? I mean, how does it come about? How can we approach it? How is it apprehended?

It may be apprehended through the means of grace, e.g., Bible, prayer, worship, fellowship and witness. By prayer and with thanksgiving we make our request known to God. Disciple making is very structured, but it, very importantly, is not programmatic. That is, there are fundamentals and processes, but without exception, it is always dependent upon the Holy Spirit.

We desire to be found faithful! But we know from our own experience that the enemy, the demands of our culture, and our own sin nature tend to have a taut grip upon us and we are no match for them by ourselves. Therefore, dependency on the Lord and accountability to each other is imperative.

Therefore, it is necessary and essential to recalibrate our spiritual compass, find our bearings in Scripture and pursue holiness. We know from Scripture that without holiness, no man [woman or child] shall see God. "And you will seek Me and find Me, when you search for Me with all your heart," Jeremiah 29:13. "You shall not have any other gods before Me," Exodus 20:3. "...For I, the Lord your God, am a jealous God," Exodus 20:5.

Relationship, fellowship, Bible study, discipleship, prayer, worship, stewardship, mentoring, availability, accountability, evangelism and short-term missions are all building blocks that strengthen the disciple and the disciple maker. These building blocks or elements are interrelated and are necessary for our growth. These building blocks are long term.

We are admonished from Scripture not to construct a building, organization, or enter into discipleship ministry without first counting the cost. "For which of you, intending to build a tower, does not sit down first and count the cost, whether he has enough to finish it…" Luke 14:28. "So likewise, whoever of you does not forsake all that he has cannot be My disciple," Luke 14:33.

 "But seek first the kingdom of God and His righteousness, and all these things shall be added to you," Matthew 6:33.

It is important to look at or examine where we are, and whether we desire to be on the path of obedience individually. We are to be Spirit–led. Jesus explained that apart from Him we could do nothing. That includes our discipleship ministry!

Look Around to See Where God is at Work?

Men, women, and children who are believers are called 'first' to be obedient to God. The world measures success in many ways. The Christian measures success in his or her obedience to the Living God. Therefore, how can I be a good son or daughter, approved of God, if I am not found in the path of obedience?

"Therefore you shall be perfect, just as your Father in heaven is perfect," Matthew 5:48. The standard is holiness. We are entirely dependent on Him, the Author and Finisher of our faith. God initiated disciple making. Therefore, it is pleasing to God, and it is always for our good.

Blackaby and King from their book, "Experiencing God", remind us, "The Holy Spirit and the Word of God will instruct you and help you know when and where God is working. Once you know where He is working, you will adjust your life to join Him where He is working," page 15. We are encouraged to look around ourselves to see where God is at work. Then we are encouraged to join Him in that work. The model is Jesus who came to do the will of His Father, to seek and to save that which was lost. "For I have come down from heaven, not to do My own will, but the will of Him who sent Me," John 6:38. "... For the Son of Man has come to seek and to save that which was lost," Luke 19:10.

Discipleship requires the study of Holy Scripture to show ourselves approved and to give an answer for the faith that lies within us. Discipleship carries with it the imperative to 'share the gospel' in season and out of season as a way-of-life. Even the best sermons preached among men without the gospel is at best a 'Christ–less' sermon!

The Great Commission is not an optional extra, but a way-of-life for His disciples! Are you His disciple? Are you making disciples? Ask of Him who is able to do exceeding abundantly more than you can ask or think, to first make you His disciple, and then to make you His disciple maker.

Discipleship is commanded in the Bible. It is dependent on Almighty God alone. It is to live in obedience and in a loving relationship with our Savior and Lord. May it please God to revive His Church in the United States of America for His glory and to enlarge our love for Him.

"Not everyone who says to Me, 'Lord, Lord,' shall enter the kingdom of heaven, but he who does the will of My Father in heaven," Matthew 7:21. "Therefore whoever hears these sayings of Mine, and does them, I will liken him to a wise man who built his house on the rock," Matthew 7:24.

Bibliography

Alcorn, Randy. *The Grace and Truth Paradox.* Sisters, Oregon: Multnomah Publishers, Inc., 2003

Baxter, Richard. *The Reformed Pastor.* Edinburgh, U.K.: The British Printing Company Ltd., 1994.

Blackaby, Henry T. & King, Claude V. *Experiencing God.* Nashville, Tennessee: Lifeway Press, 1984.

Davies, Eryl. *The Beddgelert Revival.* Bryntirion, Bridgend, Wales, UK: Bryntirion Press, 2004.

Edwards. Jonathan. *Jonathan Edwards on Revival.* Edinburg, U.K.: Banner of Truth Trust, 1757, 1972.

Engles, Joseph P. *First Catechism.* Sewanee, Georgia: Great Commission Publications, 1840.

Finney, Charles G. *Lectures on Revival.* Minneapolis, Minnesota: Bethany House Publishers, 1988.

Foundation for Reformation. *New Geneva Study Bible.* United States of America: Thomas Nelson, Inc., 1995.

Grubb, Norman. *C. T. Studd - Cricketer & Pioneer.* Christian Literature Crusade, Fort Washington, Pennsylvania, 1982.

Hoekema, Anthony A. *Created in God's Image.* Carlisle, UK: William B. Eerdmans Publishing Company, 1986

Hoekema, Anthony A. *The Bible and the Future.* Carlisle, UK: William B. Eerdmans Publishing Company, 1994.

Hoover, J. Edgar. *Masters of Deceit.* New York, New York: Henry Holt & Company Inc., 1958.

Jefferson, Thomas. *Declaration of Independence.* Virginia: United States Congress, 1776.

Lincoln, Abraham. *Gettysburg Address.* Gettysburg, Pennsylvania: Congressional Records, 1863

Madison, James. *The Constitution of the United States of America.* New York: United States Congress, 1887.

Murray, Iain. *Jonathan Edwards on Revival.* Carlisle, Pennsylvania: Banner of Truth Trust, 1958.

Phillips, Thomas. *The Welsh Revival.* Great Britain: BPC Paperbacks Ltd., 1989.

Pink, Arthur W. *The Attributes of God.* Grand Rapids, Michigan: Baker Book House, 2004.

Schaeffer, Francis A. *No Little People.* United States of America: InterVarsity Press, 1974.

Schaeffer, Francis A. *The Great Evangelical Disaster.* Wheaton, Illinois: Crossway Books, 2006.

Schaeffer, Francis A. *True Spirituality.* Wheaton, Illinois: Tyndale House Publishers, 1971.

Settle, Paul. *To God All Praise and Glory*. United States of America: The Presbyterian Church in America, 1998.

Smartt, Kennedy. *I Am Reminded*. Lawrenceville, Georgia: PCA Christian Education and Publication, 1998.

Wiersbe, Warren W. *With the Word*. Nashville, Tennessee: Oliver Nelson Books, 1991.

Wray, Daniel E. *Biblical Church Discipline*. Edinburgh: The Banner of Truth Trust 1978.

13200197R00091

Made in the USA
Charleston, SC
23 June 2012